PERSONNEL SECURITY VETTING

Issues and More Issues

TERRY THOMPSON, PH.D.

outskirts
press

Personnel Security Vetting:
Issues and More Issues
All Rights Reserved.
Copyright © 2020 Terry Thompson, Ph.D.
v2.0

The opinions expressed in this manuscript are solely the opinions of the author and do not represent the opinions or thoughts of the publisher. The author has represented and warranted full ownership and/or legal right to publish all the materials in this book.

This book may not be reproduced, transmitted, or stored in whole or in part by any means, including graphic, electronic, or mechanical without the express written consent of the publisher except in the case of brief quotations embodied in critical articles and reviews.

Outskirts Press, Inc.
http://www.outskirtspress.com

Paperback ISBN: 978-1-9772-2491-0

Outskirts Press and the "OP" logo are trademarks belonging to Outskirts Press, Inc.

PRINTED IN THE UNITED STATES OF AMERICA

Table of Contents

Introduction	i
One: Overview	1
Two: The Background Investigation	10
Three: Polygraph	28
Four: Adjudications	45
Five: Psychology and Personnel Security	58
Six: Personnel Security and Catastropic Events	76
Seven: Risk, Percentages, Proportionality, and Probabilities	83
Eight: Substance Use and Abuse	92
Nine: Finances	106
Ten: Other Adjudicative Issues	115
Eleven: Summary and Conclusions	131
Appendix	136
Sources	152

INTRODUCTION

Many years ago when I was a young security officer for the Central Intelligence Agency we used to have discussions about which branch of security was more important—Personnel Security or Physical Security. The discussions usually went something like this: If we put enough locks on things nobody can tamper with our classified materials—versus-- if we make certain our people are trustworthy, reliable and honest we will not need to worry about locking stuff down.

Today there is no more argument. Personnel Security has won. Today, of course, we also have Cyber Security to consider but the same rationale applies. No matter how sophisticated our cyber defenses are, a determined, cyber- sophisticated offender (like Edward Snowden) can usually find a way around those defenses. If the individual is proven to be trustworthy, however, we need not worry about our systems—they are largely safe from insider threats.

Of course this is not and should not be a bipolar conversation; we need all three types of security but Personnel Security is the most needed.

Driven largely by negligence lawsuits, some legitimate and others obviously contrived, the private sector is struggling with this issue. Screening potential employees can be costly and time consuming but doing so properly can be less expensive and time consuming than a large lawsuit.

This not a textbook designed to enunciate the particulars of PS nor is it an instruction manual. It is not a step by step *how to* book to be taught to undergraduate or undergraduate-like students. It will be a discussion of the myths and controversies, rights and wrongs and, most importantly, the reasoning pertinent to PS from one who has worked in that community for a very long time.

So what is good Personnel Security all about?

CHAPTER ONE

OVERVIEW

In its simplest form, Personnel Security (PS) is comprehensive screening of candidates for jobs and/or security clearances. This book will use the national security model of personnel security screening but the principles and techniques can be employed in the private sector as well. They are also equally applicable to the decision to grant or deny a security clearance or suitability for employment. To simplify the discussion and to make this book germane to the private sector, I will speak largely in terms of employment decisions. PS requires an in-depth examination of a person's past and present to determine if he/she is a good risk for the future.

What that amounts to is prediction of future behavior. Given the complexities of human behavior and the interaction of environmental factors with psychic instincts, such predictions are high risk indeed. Success cannot be defined as Ted Williams batting average was; he failed two out of three times at bat but was the best hitter in the history of baseball. No, our definition of success must be considerably better than that.

Actually, our decisions are really risk based probabilities—as are most decisions. Indeed the PS equation is based solely on risk, probabilities and percentages. Given the difficulty of the task, and the potentially enormous impact of being wrong, our task takes on risk that is potentially larger than life.

Aaron Alexis, the Navy Yard shooter killed 12 people in a random shooting in 2013. Alexis held a SECRET security clearance at the time and displayed fairly clear signs of a psychological disorder immediately prior to the shooting. He was hearing voices, reacting to those voices and deteriorating rapidly. He was quoted, *Ultra low frequency attack is what I've been subject to for the last 3 months. And to be perfectly honest, that is what has driven me to this.* [1] As always, after a case like this the question arises as to what was observable, what was known, what should have been known and was the tragedy preventable? Implicitly or explicitly the question takes the form of-- should the personnel security screening system have alerted someone to this potential catastrophe? (The truth is that the people who were aware of his mental health issues, for reasons that are not clear, did not report his disordered behavior to the right government sources) [2]

This case perfectly illustrates the risk now commonly associated with **insider threat** i.e. someone already cleared or hired who is supposed to be a trusted insider yet engages in some unacceptable act like a mass shooting. In most of these cases, the individual was previously vetted and adjudged to be trustworthy. In a majority of those cases the vetting was acceptable and the individual was indeed trustworthy at the time; the personnel security screening was adequate but the individual changed over the years and devolved into a high threat person. This is particularly true when screening younger subjects, usually ages 18 through the mid-30s. Most of us have undergone substantial change

---

[1] Greg Botelho and Joe Sterling.. *FBI: Navy Yard shooter 'delusional,' said 'low frequency attacks' drove him to kill.* CNN September 26, 2013, Retrieved 17 July 2017. https://edition.cnn.com/2013/09/25/us/washington-navy-yard-investigation/

[2] Internal review of the Washington Navy Yard Shooting, A Report to the Secretary of Defense, 20 Nov, 2013, Retrieved, 17 July 2019, P 3. https://apps.dtic.mil/dtic/tr/fulltext/u2/a602573.pdf

in these early years while the later years tend to be more static—at least in terms of character and trustworthiness. Our basic values are largely established by the 30s (often much sooner.)

The insider threat is now thought of as THE threat because, obviously, this person already has access to our buildings, our information and our IT systems. He/she is in a much better position to cause harm or damage by virtue of his nearness to vital assets. For this reason, this book will focus primarily on the insider threat.

In the Alexis case, he held a SECRET clearance which gave him an access badge which gave him unfettered access to the building where he killed 12 of his fellow employees. Armed guards prevented persons without a badge from entry into the building thereby providing an ostensible safe space for employees. Absent the clearance and badge he undoubtedly could have started shooting outside the building but the impacts likely would have been less. It was likewise with Nidal Hassan, the Fort Hood shooter who had unrestrained access to a military base where he too shot and killed numerous coworkers.

The critical question relative to cases like these is: Were they improperly vetted initially or did life change them after the vetting? Many individuals gain a clearance or a job and sometimes remain in that capacity for 30 years or more. This timeframe provides a great deal of opportunity for life to change a person and often not for the better. Divorce, drug and/or alcohol abuse, financial strains and psychological stress, to name a few, often visit us at different times in life. In these two cases it seems apparent that changes occurred after the initial grant of a security clearance. In other cases, like the spy Aldridge Ames, there were observables that should have been alerting. (He owned a house worth $650,000 ((in 1985)) with no mortgage.) [3]

It is also important to note the unavoidable tension implicit in any

---

[3] Earley, P (1997) Confessions of a Spy, Putnam & Sons, NY, P 261

PS screening effort. On one hand we have comprehensiveness. Our efforts should be all inclusive and extensively investigated so that we can accumulate a maximum amount of knowledge for an adjudicative determination. No stone should be left unturned and the more we know about our subject the better.

Conversely, the information development stage cannot be overly invasive. For example, a primary investigative focus is in the area of financial posture. Does an individual have too many debts which would make her vulnerable to coercion or financial crimes? Does she have unexplained affluence i.e. does she NOT have debts that are normal to her financial status in life and if so, why not? Some spies, like Brian Regan, attempted to hide his debt by placing it in his spouse's name. Should the investigative body do a full investigation on a spouse? Or is that too invasive?

Should the investigative organization delve deeply into one's sex life? After all, it seems like every day we see cases of clearly unacceptable sexual behavior rise to surface. The cases of Jeffrey Epstein and Harvey Weinstein offer substantial testimony to this need. Or does it? [4]

This tension is pervasive and never ending. I have been involved in many meetings trying to determine what these guidelines ought to be and to what extent they should be pursued and the challenges are endless. In the interest of being non-invasive we may choose to be less than comprehensive but what if some potentially alerting factor is missed? We may subsequently be open to criticism for missing some potentially predictive factor.

Suppose we are investigating John Q. Smith and we have no suspicion

---

[4] In the Intelligence Community, we no longer aggressively pursue the topic of sexuality but accept and adjudicate what readily comes our way. For example, arrests for sexual crimes are a reasonable segue to a follow up investigation. Absent a pre-existing flag, the issues of sexuality (non-criminal) are essentially ignored.

of sexual wrongdoing. Should we simply pursue sexual inquiries on everyone because a few may be in the Jeffrey Epstein category? This would certainly address the comprehensiveness issue but is it too invasive?

How about social media accounts? The subject of an investigation signs a consent form giving us access to her records. Should we completely explore all of her social media postings? Is that properly comprehensive or too invasive? The reader in now welcome to the real world of Personnel Security.

Some Monday morning quarterbacks, often journalists, do not live in the real world; after all they are largely in the business of finding some shortcoming and magnifying it to the public in pursuit of career goals. They evaluate someone else's work without ever having lived in those shoes—at least in most cases. That is not to say there are not many serious journalists out there uncovering real malfeasance nor is it to say that a free press is not vital to a democracy. It is. With the enormous increase in press coverage via the 24 hour news cycle, however and the proliferation of online news outlets, the rush to news has contaminated a portion of the industry. Teddy Roosevelt's quote is illuminating:

"It is not the critic who counts, not the man who points out how the strong man stumbles or where the doer of deeds could have done them better. The credit belongs to the man who is actually in the arena, whose face is marred by dust and sweat and blood, who strives valiantly but comes up short again and again because there is no effort without error and shortcoming; but who does actually strive to do the deeds; who knows great enthusiasm, the great devotions; who spends himself in a worthy cause; who, at best, knows the triumph of high achievement and who, at worst, if he fails at least fails while daring greatly so that his place will never be with those cold and timid souls who know neither victory nor defeat." [5]

Not to be too dramatic-- but we experience this kind of Monday morning quarterbacking in the Personnel Security arena. To give but one example, in the espionage case of the previously mentioned Aldridge Ames, the media created a circus over the fact that he owned a $60,000 Jaguar. [6] I have already indicated that the IC did indeed miss what should have been an alert—his house with no mortgage so I am no shill for CIA. The media, however, made it so simple—anyone with a half brain should have noted that he had a Jaguar therefore he was a potential spy. The Director of Security for CIA testified at the time that CIA employees owned lots of Jaguars and if we investigate all of them we would be wasting our time. Nowhere was that factoid reported in the media.

In Roberta Wohlstetter's brilliant book on Pearl Harbor she concluded that indeed there were suggestive signals of the attack but they were inundated by "noise" i.e. lots of other bits of intelligence which camouflaged those with predictive value. [7] In other words it is quite easy to investigate and focus on a particular incident or person i.e. if we have lead information that Jose Ramirez MAY be a terrorist the investigation that singularly focuses on him is less prone to noise interference.

Compare that to screening-- which is the definition of Personnel Security. The Intelligence Community has over four million clearances; the trick is to identify the one or two percent that may represent a substantial threat and to do so in advance of any untoward activity. Given both the complexity and fluidity of human behavior, the task is nearly impossible.

---

5 https://www.bing.com/images/search?q=teddy+roosevelt+quotes+arena&qs=CustomSearch&pq=teddy+roosevelt+quotes&sc=3-22&cvid=ADB8674BD43245A499CBA820BA0C48BA&sp=3&form=QBIR

6 Weiner, Tim; Johnston, David; Lewis, Neil A. (1995). Betrayal: *The Story of Aldrich Ames, An American Spy*. New York: Random House. P 145

7 Wohlstetter, R, (1962) *Pearl Harbor: Warning and Decision*, Stanford University Press, CA.

Wohlstetter's theory of noise, now accepted by virtually all intelligence scholars, is absolutely critical to real world understanding of PS. Hindsight eliminates all noise and seems to make personnel security screening easy. This is not the real world.

The government field of PS has undergone gradual but substantial changes over the last 40 years but the basic issue of size and the resulting complexity is unchanged. In a phrase, personnel security screening is extraordinarily difficult. While it is true that most insiders who "go bad" do not engage in espionage, mass shootings or mass leaking. No, most of them become problematic employees and generate a substantial amount of managerial and security problems. Some, however, do engage in mass leaking (Edward Snowden) mass shootings Nidal Hassan and/or espionage (Robert Hanssen.) The problematic employees we can live with, the spies, mass shooters and mass leakers we cannot.

Another core issue of PS screening is the notion that past behavior may be predictive of future behavior. This assumption is the core supposition in James Fitzgerald's book, *Journey to the Center of the Mind* wherein he explores the psyche of serial killers. He maintains that past behavior is the closest tool we have to evaluate risk for future undesirable behavior. [8] PS makes the same assumption but obviously within a different milieu. To the extent this is true it is particularly helpful when evaluating **recent** behavior. I will discuss this further in the chapter on background investigations but here I want to address the validity of this assumption.

In a study of espionage done in 2006, this researcher compared a population of known spies who were interviewed in depth after their espionage with a population of other cleared members of the IC who did not commit espionage. The matched pairs approach was used i.e. gender, age and other factors were used. So a 20-30 year old white

---

8 Fitzgerald, J, (2014) *Journey to the Center of the Mind*, West Conshohocken, PA.

male spy with a security clearance was compared to another 20-30 white male non-spy. The comparison entailed some of the risk factors employed in PS screening: finances, drugs, alcohol abuse, crime and emotional issues. The examination focused on pre-espionage behaviors.

The outcomes were illuminating. Emotional issues were 11 times more prevalent in spies than non-spies, financial issues 4x, drugs and alcohol abuse 3x and crime substantially more present in the spy population than the non-spies. [9] These data inform the PS screening process and offer hard evidence that the presence of certain risk factors does indeed increase the probability that untoward outcomes such as espionage may occur.

This needs to be placed in context, however. While risk factors increase the probability of undesirable ends it is nonetheless true that the vast majority of individuals who present with these risks factors will NOT commit espionage. Using hypothetical numbers, populations with risk factors may produce .001% who turn out to be spies but only .0001% of non-risk factor population will turn to espionage. So the probability factor is increased but it is still the case that almost all of risk factor population will not become spies. (The research did not examine for other undesirable outcomes like employment disciplinary measures, terminations, financial malfeasance etc. where I suspect we would see more bad results.)

While I will spend some time in this book discussing the particulars of investigations, adjudications, polygraphs and interviews, the backbone of PS, I will spend an equal amount of time on explaining the intellectual underpinnings of these techniques. In essence, I will discuss the **why** of PS screening—something that lacks clarity in the media and elsewhere.

---

9 Thompson, T (2006) *Why Espionage Happens*, Seaboard Press, Florence SC, First edition, P295-296

I will end this introduction with an anecdote.

About 25 years ago I was a member of a security board whose design was to hold open meetings for the public so that real communication and two way feedback could be accomplished. A fairly well know media member who was constantly critical of the government security community came to our first meeting, left halfway through and never returned to subsequent meetings. I must admit, our meetings were rather mundane as we grappled with routine but important real world problems. I should also add, we did not discover any earth shattering solutions. Such is the struggle for truth.

It seemed pretty apparent, however, that my media acquaintance was only interested in headlines; the real day to day work held no interest for him, save a big splash of failure which could adorn his front page.

CHAPTER TWO

THE BACKGROUND INVESTIGATION

The basic tools of Personnel Security are the background investigation (BI), polygraph (only employed by certain agencies and banned in some private sector applications) and the adjudication. The BI is the universally employed, primary tool used to develop information on an applicant. [10] It is a combination of interviews and record checks followed by a final report made to an adjudicator for a final decision.

As previously discussed the underlying premise of personnel security screening is that past behavior is predictive of future behavior. This is true most often but very often it is not. So why do we rely on something that is less than scientifically precise? Shouldn't all our processes be supported by pure scientific data? I raise this point early on because if there were scientifically precise data available to perfectly predict future behavior, we most assuredly would rely on it. Such data do not exist so we are stuck relying on these imperfect tools because that is all we have. Does the absence of a perfect BI toolkit argue for abolition of the remaining methodology? Of course not. We have

---

10 The term "applicant" will be used throughout this book to refer to one applying for job, private sector or government, or a security clearance

cameras in banks to deter and detect bank robberies but we still have bank robberies. Should we outlaw cameras because they do not work ALL the time? Obviously not. We do the best we can with what we have and as soon as a PS panacea is developed, I will call the reader. (This notion is more prominently associated with polygraph which I will discuss in a later chapter.)

The background investigation can be short and not very comprehensive (and hence less expensive) or more thorough, more expensive and more time consuming. Again, I will focus on the most comprehensive model and the reader may pare down the application in accordance the company's needs.

The model includes verification of birth, citizenship, education, criminal record, financial status, residences, court actions, FINCEN check and a subject interview.[11] There are several ways to retrieve this information. The old fashion way is to employ investigators to visit sites where these data are available, use of U.S postal service to obtain available data and/ or electronic retrieval of information where possible and practical. Which retrieval methods are best? The answer is—it depends.

The obvious trend is to collect as much data as possible via electronic sources. This is much quicker and more efficient than the shoe leather approach. What used to take a three hour round trip to a local police department for a routine criminal record check can now be accomplished, in some cases, in five minutes. Credit reporting collection is done almost entirely via electronic communication and some education verifications can also be done electronically. The benefits are both large and self-evident requiring no further description here.

The most impacting example of electronic collection is the Intelligence

---

11 Henderson, W, *Security Clearance Investigations Process Updated,* 9 Oct 2011, Clearance Jobs, Retrieved 23 July 2019, https://news.clearancejobs.com/2011/10/09/security-clearance-investigations-process-updated/

Community's Continuous Evaluation (CE) effort which is currently in the incubation phase. This endeavor capitalizes on existing databases such as the FBI NCIC database, the Treasury Department's FINCEN listing cash transactions of $10,000 or more and the terrorist databases used by the Department of Homeland Security—to name a few. This is truly "automatic" collection in that the databases can be queried on a daily basis without human initiation. It works something like this.

John Smith gets arrested for a DUI on 2 January 2019. He wants to conceal this information from his employer for obvious reasons so he does not self-report to his company security officer. In our current government system of five year reinvestigation cycle, he may have up to five years to concoct a plan to somehow minimize or further conceal his arrest. For example, if his arrest occurred in Anycounty, Utah and he has never been there before or since, the arrest may escape the normal background investigation. [12]

Under a system including CE a daily run of arrest data would not only bring this to the surface but it would do so in near real time. More importantly, John Smith would know this and hence see little point in not providing a full, real time report to his employer. His employer then has a perfect opportunity to debrief Smith and place the incident in context. Smith tells his employer this incident occurred after a New Year's Eve party and he otherwise drinks very little—a plausible explanation given the date. Essentially the event can be resolved at the time of occurrence thereby saving everyone time, money and a great deal of angst. In addition, the mere presence of a CE system may amplify the notion of deterrence and result in less undesirable behavior.

Compare this to Smith not reporting the incident at the time of occurrence and it coming to light five years later in a reinvestigation effort. In this case, Smith has compounded the impact of the incident by his

---

[12] Police checks in background investigations usually include only areas where the subject has lived, worked or gone to school.

non-reporting and cast some doubt on his overall integrity and honesty—the backbone of any PS determination.

There is much discussion in the field as to whether CE will be, or should be, a replacement for the BI or a supplement to it. Given the rapidity and accuracy of CE there is enormous pressure to expand its use and either replace or minimize the BI. To do this would be a grave mistake. Right now the IC is using CE to temporarily displace the BI so that the community can eliminate its backlog of periodic reinvestigation cases—a reasonable temporary measure which I hope does not become permanent.

While I am an enthusiastic supporter of CE, there is no substitute for talking to a **person** to get a real feel for who the subject is. No database can tell you about a person's core values or their skill set. It cannot tell whether this person has interpersonal skills, is persistent and dogged in pursuing a goal and/or is compassionate in dealing with a population of employees—to name but a few shortcomings of CE. Moreover, a database can alert us to an arrest for criminal behavior but it cannot advise us of a crime for which one has not been identified or apprehended—as a polygraph can do. CE cannot put its name on the line and recommend an individual for a trusted position as a reference can, nor can it advise of an expensive vacation taken inside the U.S. It cannot uncover undetected domestic violence-- as a neighbor can sometimes do. It cannot speak to a person's former supervisor and determine the real description of a person's work product. It cannot advise whether someone is in the process of radicalizing—as is infrequently but occasionally the case with sources close to a subject.

The last point I would like to make about CE is that it is rarely dispositive. In almost all cases it functions as an alert system. For example, CE may uncover an arrest for Criminal Mischief but that category can cover anything from graffiti to gunfire. This is particularly true in cases where there is a plea deal where pleading to a lesser offense is almost always a part of the deal. A record check alone could be drastically misleading. In almost all cases an investigator must follow up in person and speak to several people to clarify and contextualize the issue. In the aforementioned Alexis case he advised an interviewer that he had a dispute with two individuals and he let the air out of their tires—a completely true statement. He did not state, however, that he did so by firing a Glock pistol into the tires.[13]

It has yet to be determined exactly how CE will be employed—as a subset of an investigation or as an independent element of PS. Either way it will fundamentally change PS for the better but, in any event, it should not and cannot replace the BI.

One of the core suppositions of the background investigation is that talking to people who know the subject and have interacted with her can be illuminating as to the subject's character, moral fiber and trustworthiness. Furthermore, if one can reliably be described as trustworthy the probability is high that this person is a good risk for a position of trust.

Notice I use the term, *probability,* because that is what we are dealing with-not scientific precision. Too often in our rush to be, *scientific,* we reject what are perhaps our best alternatives because they are scientifically short of perfection. Other than in the hard sciences, if we only employ techniques that are 100% accurate and reliable we would have no techniques at all. And how scientific is that? Welcome to the real world.

In a typical background investigation we may interview 10 sources who know the subject to varying degrees. If at all possible, it is important to get a cross-section of sources so that we gain exposure to all aspects of the subject's life. A priest or minister may know nothing about

---

13 Homicide Watch, DOD Report 18 March 2014, *Navy Yard Shooting: DOD Missed Warning Signs, Report Says*, Retrieved 29 July, 2019, http://homicidewatch.org/2014/03/18/navy-yard-shooting-dod-missed-warning-signs-report-says/

a subject's use of marijuana in college but may be keenly aware of other shortcomings through non-confidential conversations with the subject. A college roommate may be fully cognizant of drug use but know nothing about subject's chronic tardiness at work. An ideal BI may include, for example, two high school references (a teacher and another student) two college sources (a professor and a co-student) supervisors from two or more employments and two references from each of those employers.

The BI is designed to cover all aspects of a subject's life because we all have "compartments" of behavior. We show one persona at work, a slightly different one at our children's little league game and yet another at happy hour on Friday night. This is not unnatural nor is it particularly threatening from a Personnel Security perspective-- especially if this compartmented behavior is not extreme. Nonetheless, this is one primary reason that the BI is designed to cover all aspects one's life. We all know someone who appears to be completely well-adjusted but seems to turn into a different person at happy hour or at their eight year old's soccer game. For this reason, not covering one compartment can be damaging and risks violating the Whole Person Concept. What is the Whole Person Concept?

This is the notion that the entirety of the person should be evaluated—both the good and the bad and it should be done in context and proportionality. Bad behavior ought to be examined in light of potentially aggravating versus mitigating factors. For example, if one presents a battle with alcohol emanating from the death of a loved one, this constitutes an obvious alerting factor. If, however, the subject has become an active member of AA for the past five years (since the event occurred) and has remained 100% abstinent, both the time factor and the AA treatment may mitigate the original alcohol issue. Hence this person may be a good risk for hiring. A more comprehensive discussion of the adjudication equation and the Whole Person Concept will be discussed in the later chapter on adjudications.

The reader may be asking the obvious question: Won't people lie to protect their friends in the investigative process? The answer is a resounding—yes. Ergo, we use various techniques to minimize that effect.

First we ask ALL interviewees if they would recommend the subject for a position of trust and may we attach their name to that recommendation. It is easy to lie anonymously but when placing one's name to one's comments, including a recommendation, the lying becomes a little more difficult. In addition, we do not rely only on those individuals whose names the subject has provided to us—the so called listed references. We also seek out sources NOT recommended by the subject. For example, when interviewing a supervisor at an employment we may ask her who else knew Jon and where could I find that person. Indeed, many background service providers require only one listed reference with all the remaining sources to be developed during the investigation. This is done because of the obvious; applicants will only list individuals as references who they believe will only provide positive comments to the investigator. Lastly, most investigators receive some behavioral analysis training to detect lies during interviews and they can construct reasonable follow up questions based on that analysis. Despite these measures, however, some sources will still lie but that is one of the reasons we maximize the number of people interviewed. It is unlikely ALL sources will lie or exaggerate.

Another core concept embedded in the BI is the notion of recency of behavior. Recent behavior is thought to be much more suggestive of future behavior. If a thirty five year old male is known to have smoked marijuana once per week in high school but has been abstinent for 15 years that drug use will almost certainly be tolerated in the adjudication. Had the drug use regularly occurred only six months before the adjudication, it would, in all likelihood, be grounds for disapproval—particularly for a 35 year old.

Background investigations generally look for recent PATTERNS of behavior rather than individual events. They do this for same reason i.e. patterns of behavior, as compared to singular events, are more likely to be predictive of future conduct. This is even more likely in those over 30-35 as those undesirable patterns are already more likely firmly embedded in the psyche. This person may well be past the stage of youthful experimentation and habit or addiction prevails.

Also, when conducting reference interviews we attempt to interview the best possible sources i.e. references who have known the subject longer and who have a substantial relationship.

Having done BIs myself for five years I was always struck by just how clear a picture of someone we got after talking to 10 or more people with exposure to the subject. If the subject receives 10 unqualified recommendations, that is a powerful inducement to hire/clear that individual. Although it is obviously imperfect, it is reasonable to assume a thorough background investigation will all but guarantee a higher percentage of quality people in the firm and eliminate the truly high risk individual.

To this point I have discussed initial BIs and not addressed the reinvestigation or periodic reinvestigation (PR). PRs are abbreviated BIs with less extensive coverage. There is no point in investigating things that have already been resolved (prior education, employments etc.) so the PR functions to bring up to date an existing PS case. If the subject has had an additional education or employment after the initial BI that is confirmed in the PR. The PR also requires references, both listed and developed, as a part of the endeavor.

PRs are **always** a lower priority than initial background investigations. In initial cases the subject has not yet gone to work and thus an inherent pressure exists to get this person working and producing for the company. Whereas the employee who is already working presents no loss of productivity and, as a general proposition, has no time sensitivity associated with his case. The PR can be 6 -9-12 months later and no consequences will be felt. I should say no consequences will be felt **in almost all cases**. Moreover, the current employee has already been investigated and adjudicated so the risk factor for him is deemed to be much less. This is true **in almost all cases.**

The problem with this train of thought is two-fold. While it is certainly true that the previously vetted employee is less likely to be a security problem, when she does present a problem it can have an enormous impact and be the most difficult to resolve.

This employee already has access to sensitive information and company assets. She can destroy electronic infrastructure, sell/provide proprietary company information to a competitor or shoot up the office space. In addition, if something serious arises on the PR we may be removing this person's means of livelihood—a catastrophic outcome for most who experience this. Dismissal of an employee is, obviously, an extreme event and may embitter the former employee to the extent she may seek revenge. Most often that revenge is non-violent and legal, sometimes it is not.

Edward Howard was an employee of CIA who was fired for illegal drug use and thefts while in access. These issues were compounded by Howard's ongoing, chronic drinking problem. [14] Howard was a case officer i.e. one who actually recruits assets usually in an overseas environment and who think of themselves as the elite corps of C.I.A. (Just for the record the other components think THEY are the elite) Howard was slated to transfer to Moscow when he was scheduled to take a polygraph and failed the test while making damaging admissions. He was subsequently fired and eventually defected to Moscow where he became a reporting asset providing classified information to the

---

14 Wise, D. (1988) *The Spy Who Got Away*, Random House, NY, P 73 & 81.

KGB. [15] Howard's motivation was primarily revenge seeking against the CIA. [16] He is the apotheosis of a revenge seeker driven by the ultimate PS action—termination.

The PS lesson learned from this case was employees who are dismissed for cause must be very delicately managed. Since almost all employment terminations are traumatic the employee's reactions are usually visceral, pronounced and long lasting. They provide ample grounds for the harshest of emotions and a wish for revenge. Hence a "soft landing" should be constructed each case. Depending on the facts of the case, this soft landing may include a generous package of benefits to include severance pay, temporary medical benefits, counseling and assistance in gaining new employment.

This may strike the reader as grossly unfair; why should someone who clearly engaged in severely untoward behavior be rewarded with such benefits? The reader is correct—depending on the facts of the case this is usually unfair. Conversely, in many cases the former employee may simply be a bad fit for the company and probably should not have been hired in the first place—perhaps an HR failure. In any event, I dare say most dismissed employees are largely to blame for their plight but they are nonetheless not evil people. In addition, from a practical perspective the company must consider whether the terminated employee presents a risk for a minimal adverse issue like bad public relations or to a maximal issue like a mass shooting. There also many unfavorable outcomes in between these two extremes. Is providing a soft landing just plain good business while at the same time showing some compassion for one who is in a very difficult position?

The Periodic Reinvestigation interval in the Intelligence Community has almost always been five years. That has been the goal but in reality overdue PRs have been commonly observed to last as long at ten

---

15 Ibid, P131
16 Ibid P255

years. This is usually due to resource shortages—BIs and full screening of employees can be expensive and are necessarily lower priority than initials. As previously stated, this is because initials enable people to get hired and get to work while PRs have no such obstacle attached to them.

Here is the problem with low priority PRs—we are de-prioritizing the very threat that everyone agrees is the penultimate issue of the day i.e. the insider threat. While recognizing the prevalence and intensity of the insider threat we are nonetheless de-escalating one of our best tools to combat it—the PR. The outsider poses considerably less threat to the company/agency than the insider yet we consistently delay PRs.

In discussing background investigations we must distinguish between what are productive sources and what are not. There are two potential elements of productivity: quantitative sources and qualitative sources. Quantitative sources provide a greater volume of information while qualitative sources provide more useful information. The bottom line question is who/what sources produce the most amount of useful information.

For example, does a neighborhood investigation dating back seven years provide as much solid information as a more recent employment? Does an interview with a college professor dating back to seven years ago produce the same quality/quantity of useful data as a current developed reference? The answer is almost always no to both questions but, in reality, the answer is: it depends.

Based on my own experience as an investigator, I can say with high confidence, that most college professors have fleeting and superficial contacts with their undergraduate students. Most often they can refer to a record and confirm attendance and grade but further insight is unusual. The relationship with graduate students tends to be more substantive but is still lacking in long lasting depth.

Of course, if the investigator just happens to hit the student who was a straight A, had superb interpersonal skills, produced a most unusual and impacting research project and was a recent student, chances are much better that the investigator's time will be well-spent. As a general rule, however, investigators tend not to waste a lot of time trying to locate college professors with an in-depth knowledge of the subject because they know that effort is unlikely to produce quality returns.

Conversely, a listed reference will almost always know the subject well and will produce a volume of data. Often they have a long history of varied experiences with the subject and can talk at length about that history. The problem may well be the quality of information is often sub-optimal. The subject and reference are obviously friends and ergo the reference is almost always reluctant to provide derogatory information. So the quality of data, despite the length and depth of the relationship, may well be less than helpful. It is up to the investigator to make a determination as to quality and credibility of information provided and note that in her report.

Without a doubt, the most prolific source of information in a background investigation is derived from the subject interview (SI). One study concluded that the subject himself provided issue information in 81% of the cases and that 97.6% of the issue cases were developed within a 7-year scope. [17] So, in this instance the data are current and voluminous. Once again, and perhaps more so than a listed reference interview, the source of the information (the subject himself) is certainly biased.

Since the subject knows everything about himself, it certainly makes sense that the SI would be the most productive source. The interviewer

---

17 *Enhanced the Productivity and Scope of Background Investigations (1996, 1991)* PERSEREC, Monterey CA. Retrieved 4 August 2019, https://www.dhra.mil/PERSEREC/Past-Achievements/#BIs

usually uses the application documents (in the IC the SF 86) as a basis for the SI. Minor issues, typos and good faith errors can be rectified before the investigation and hence a great deal of shoe leather may be preserved. Often the SI is done AFTER the investigation is completed and gaps, shortcomings and errors clarified at that point to finalize the investigation. Either time point may be used and it may vary from case to case. There is no government policy mandating one or the other.

Obviously, the subject has a vested interest in providing only positive information while minimizing or concealing derogatory information. Almost anyone applying for a job will do this. Sometimes this equates to out-and-out lying but most often it includes omissions, distortions and/or exaggerations. The subject is **not** assumed to be telling the truth and the primary reason a BI consists of multiple sources is to confirm truths and alert Personnel Security officials to inconsistencies demanding further investigation or a follow up subject interview.

The use of polygraph as a complement to the BI is a substantial incentive for truth telling. Unfortunately, the Employment Polygraph Protection Act (EPPA) prohibits most use of polygraphs for employment screening by the private sector. (The government, as usual, exempts itself from the act) Exceptions are made, however, for certain types of employment-- to wit armored car drivers, guard services, alarm technicians and pharmaceutical firms. [18] I shall discuss this more in the later chapter on polygraph.

Dating back to the 70s, SI interviews were specifically prohibited. The thinking was that the investigator may develop bias, either positive or negative, toward the subject and taint the investigation. This changed as experience showed that the SI was maximally productive. At a minimum, the SI better focuses investigative resources in implementation of the BI. At a maximum it helps to uncover wrongdoing and

---

18 U.S. Department of Labor Web Page, Wage and Hour Division, Employee Polygraph Protection Act (EPPA) Overview, Retrieved 5 Aug 2019, https://www.dol.gov/whd/polygraph/

deception.

Another recent innovation in the background investigation is the former spouse interview. The reader's immediate response is likely one of disbelief i.e. wouldn't a former spouse be the least credible source imaginable? The answer, in many cases, is yes but that does not mean that ex-spouses cannot provide solid data.

For example, suppose we want to confirm (or re-confirm) dates of employment and circumstances of resignation. In today's litigious environment many, if not most HR departments, release very minimal data—and the release often excludes whether the employee is eligible for rehire. This is a critical datum in an investigation and is strongly suggestive of the quality of work performed. If the ex-spouse states the subject is NOT eligible for rehire and further states he was forced to resign for performance reasons, we have learned a great deal. Of course, we do NOT take the word of the former spouse but rather we pursue this point with additional investigation. Most likely we would obtain additional sources familiar with the employment, like coworkers, to confirm the conditions of resignation.

Similarly, if the ex-spouse advises subject worked at the ABC Company and the subject did not include that employment on her application form, we have once again learned a great deal. The investigator would then proceed to ABC Company to confirm.

Occasionally a former spouse will provide objective data with little opportunity for bias. Dates of residence at an older neighborhood are a primary example of an instance offering little opportunity for an ex-spouse to prevaricate. He/she may think that there are records available to confirm dates of residence and ergo be reluctant to falsify this information. Moreover, there is usually no reason to misrepresent these dates and hence the information is likely more credible but, as always, subject to further investigation and confirmation.

It should also be noted that, in some cases, the opposite incentive exists. If, for example, an ex-wife is receiving alimony and child support payments from her ex-husband, the last thing she may want is to have her ex-husband lose his job and jeopardize her income. In such cases the ex-spouse may have a strong incentive to hide shortcomings of the ex-spouse.

In sum, the ex-spouse can be a source of voluminous data but that data must be critically evaluated. Most divorces are unpleasant affairs and some extremely so. Divorces usually have high emotional equities (feelings of love, betrayal, children, etc.) and often high financial equities like money and housing. These conditions tend to promote raw emotions which are fertile ground for subjective, inaccurate and arrantly falsified information. Ergo the information derived has a high potential for bias and must be considered accordingly.

The practice of interviewing ex-spouses derived largely from one of the worst spy cases in the post WWII era—the John Walker case. In this case Walker, a Navy man with a Top Secret clearance, was selling classified information to the Soviet Union. He did this initially as active duty and later as a retiree and the information was cryptological in nature thereby allowing our adversaries to decode navy military messaging-- to include scheduling of flights over North Vietnam. This information may have been responsible for the shooting down of some of our pilots over Vietnam. [19]

As any counterintelligence officer can attest, the initial identification of a spy is the most difficult part of the process. With over four million security clearances in the U.S. government, the identification of a single spy represents a daunting task indeed. It is tantamount to finding the proverbial needle in a haystack.

In the Walker case, his wife Barbara, notified the FBI that her husband

---

[19] Earley, P, (1988) *Family of Spies*, Bantam Books, NY, P 129

was a spy. John was 10k behind in his alimony payments and Barbara claimed he had a houseboat, a plane and a young girlfriend. The FBI was initially skeptical thinking perhaps this was a spurned woman seeking revenge-- but eventually followed up.[20] Thus the most damaging spy in post WWII history was identified, investigated, charged and sentenced to life imprisonment based, in part, on the report of a former spouse. This case was not the only stimulus for the adoption of former spouse interviews in BIs but it was certainly a substantial part of the impetus.

To this point, with the exception of Continuous Evaluation (CE), I have focused on the interview portion of the BI. That is because it is, in my judgment, the most important part of the process. A database may tell us someone was arrested for petty assault but that is not contextually dispositive. A police officer, a prosecutor or a witness can tell us if the charge was made by one drunken friend against another drunken friend and quickly dropped the next day or was an attack with a knife pled down to petty assault.

Nonetheless record checks are crucial to the process and start with confirmation of birth and citizenship which confirms the person is who he says he is. This is particularly germane in today's cyber world where identity theft is commonplace. Likewise, records can provide hard data which tends to speak to performance as with GPA in high school or college. School disciplinary records and credit reports are also illuminating as are civil court records. Once again these record checks must be placed in context by a person familiar with the issue. In this fashion record checks and relevant interviews are complementary and together form the basis for the BI.

New to the field of Personnel Security is the phenomenon of social media. To what extent, if any, should social media posts be explored as part of a BI? The current regulations allow for full review of any social media content that is publically available. Other sources requiring

---

20 Ibid, P 347

passwords or other defensive devices may not be examined nor may the investigative authority request such access. [21] This practice is contradictory to the previously stated dogma of examining past behavior to predict future behavior. Here we have someone **saying** something that we may take into account in the adjudication. Of course the principle of informing PS judgments based on behavior does not preclude examining what a person says or posts. Both can provide useful data for analysis but the old axiom of actions speak louder than words still predominates.

For example the Florida Parkland shooter, Nikolas Cruz posted a statement that he would become a school shooter. He posted this **before** the shooting occurred and much was made of this i.e. why didn't someone report this to law enforcement? [22] This is complicated because the shooter not only said this but took one step further posting the material. This suggests greater import and intentionality as compared to a mere utterance. High school kids across the country say things like they want to kill their English teacher or they would like to blow up the school before their math final. These statements are clearly rhetorical flourishes made by immature youths and ought not to be taken too seriously. Posting online, however, suggests some premeditation. The material observed on social media can and should be used as lead information requiring follow up investigation.

It is appropriate here to make a clear distinction between PS screening investigations and criminal investigations. In criminal investigations there is some form of evidence, often minimal, which justifies a further look at an individual. Cruz's posting was more than enough evidence to interview him and, if appropriate, launch follow up action. In PS screening cases there is usually no such evidence and we are examining a large population for the presence of risk factors. Usually these risk

---

21 Security Executive Agent Directive 5, Clapper, J, 12 May 2016. P 3.
22 Wells G. & Needleham, S, Florida Shooter: When Social Media Foretells a Mass Shooting, Wall Street Journal, 16 Feb 2018, Retrieved 12 Aug 2019, https://www.wsj.com/articles/when-social-media-foretells-a-mass-shooting-1518802803

factors are presented via behavior of the individual and do not constitute crimes (financial problems, educational disciplinary actions, birth records, alcohol abuse etc.)

Moreover, background investigations for PS screening are not designed to identify spies or criminals but rather to determine if a subject is a good risk for national security or a good risk for employment in the private sector. The presence of factors such a prior crime or mishandling of sensitive information may suggest otherwise. Occasionally a spy or a criminal will be uncovered but that is not the design. The objective is to make a risk based judgment as to a person's overall reliability, trustworthiness and integrity. If we can do that, the probability will be less that the person becomes problematic.

Since the private sector is largely prohibited from using polygraph in PS screening and several government agencies decline to employ polygraph, the BI becomes THE vehicle of information collection. Hence it is imperative the BI be performed as comprehensively and non-invasively as possible.

The current Federal Investigative Standards (FIS) may be found on the website of the Office of the Director of National Intelligence. These standards enunciate the minimum levels of coverage designed to facilitate reciprocity.

CHAPTER THREE

POLYGRAPH

Polygraph is one of the most controversial techniques used in PS screening. It is used by some of the Intelligence Community agencies for screening --with the exception of the Department of Defense. [23] As a former polygraph examiner myself, let me start by explaining what polygraph is and how it actually works; what it can do and what it cannot. Having said that, this chapter will not be a "how to" manual but rather will tackle the most controversial, and largely unaddressed, issues associated with polygraph.

First, it is not a lie detector—there is no such thing. The polygraph process uses various attachments similar to medical instruments to monitor physiological processes. Two flexible pneumograph tubes are placed around the thorax and abdomen to measure respiration rate and amplitude. A finger clip is employed to monitor sweat gland activity and a blood pressure cuff is used to observe cardio activity. The essence of the process is to measure physiological responses, or the absence of the same, in response to already reviewed questions. For example the examiner asks, "As an adult have you ever committed a crime?" Each question is asked a minimum of three times to draw conclusions.

---

23 The Defense Intelligence Agency uses polygraph for PS screening but the remainder of DOD does not.

The entire test is based on the fight or flight (or fear of consequences) principle. This theory holds that the Sympathetic Nervous System (SNS), specifically the amygdala, stimulates blood flow, cardiac response and enhanced sweat gland activity in response to the threat of discovery. When a person lies while knowing his system is being monitored and ergo his reactions will be observable, this cognizance will generate and enhance his reactivity. [24] It is a simple concept that all of us have experienced at one time or another and is the basic physiological principle undergirding polygraph.

The questions are thoroughly reviewed with the subject before the actual test. This portion, known as the pretest, is the most important part of the test. During this review the examiner reviews the definition of a crime (behavior for which you could have been arrested) and defines adult as age 18 or more. If the subject indicates she has a sensitivity to the question, that sensitivity must be explored in full.

For example, despite the fact that the examiner has made it clear that we are only concerned with behavior after the age of 18, interviewees will commonly introduce juvenile behavior. Sometimes this behavior is for a legitimate misdemeanor or felony and the subject simply must discuss it despite her knowledge that it is outside the intent of the question. Why is that?

By definition, we are measuring the reaction between body and mind and that reactivity is not always entirely rational. That is, an individual may know intellectually that a behavior is outside the thrust of the question but still feel physiologically ill at ease about it. This is quite common. Assuming the subject tells the examiner they are uncomfortable (not always the case) it is incumbent on the examiner to further discuss the issue which will result in a catharsis i.e. physical relief that can be experienced by the subject. Depending on the nature

---

[24] Abrams, S, (1989) *The Complete Polygraph Handbook*, Lexington Books, Lexington Mass. P 33

of the offense, this may take two minutes or two hours. In any case the issue must be resolved before any testing can take place. If the subject fails to advise the examiner of this anxiety in the pretest, he will almost certainly fail to get through the test. But whose fault is that? Is that a shortcoming of the polygraph process? Certainly not—the subject has failed to play by the rules.

Going back to the notion of the subject advising of his discomfort with a question in the pretest, the examiner may simply need to re-phrase the question to wit, "Are you concealing anything about criminal behavior?" Since the subject has already discussed his juvenile behavior, he is clearly not concealing it.

Let's assume no amount of discussion or question restructuring eliminates the anxiety-- also commonplace. What then? The examiner may need to structure a specialized test including, for example, questions like, Are you concealing any criminal drug behavior? Are you concealing any violent criminal activity? Are you concealing any theft? Are you concealing any other type of criminal behavior? If the subject reacts to only one question that identifies the source of concern.

Almost all laymen speak to the issue of generalized anxiety or general nervous tension (GNT) as a source of false positives i.e. truthful people being identified as untruthful. Nothing could be further from the truth. Almost everyone who undergoes a polygraph, including honest people determined to be fully forthcoming, display some level of GNT. This completely natural and is easily managed on a test.

For honest people the pretest discussion serves as a vehicle of catharsis whereby the general level of tension is reduced. Once the examiner explains the basics of the test, performs what is called an acquaintance test [25] and the subject actually feels how the test is conducted,

---

25 The subject picks a number and is then is told to lie about it on the acquaintance test. In this fashion the subject comes to know what to expect and the examiner can see how the subject's physiology is working.

most GNT dissipates. Often the subject makes some admission to some wrongdoing, minor or otherwise, and this further diminishes the anxiety.

For dishonest people, the opposite is true; as the test proceeds the tension will increase because she knows she is withholding information and the fight or flight reflex is triggered. The fact that some people attempt to lie on a polygraph is commonplace yet the mere idea seems to offend opponents. Almost everyone who has approached me about their friend's test complained of a false positive (A truth teller erroneously branded as a prevaricator.) No one ever seems to complain about a bad guy getting through—until a spy case manifests itself.

It is important to point out that in polygraph testing we measure relative changes in responsiveness to particular questions. In cases where a high level of generalized anxiety is present it is nonetheless almost always possible to observe question variations. There are some subject's that undergo testing, however, who are deemed inconclusive due to exceptionally high levels of generalized anxiety. These numbers tend to be low and these individuals tend be very high strung and are readily observable.

Another important point is that a subject's conscience, or lack thereof, is **not** a factor in a polygraph test. We do not ask a subject if he engaged in a behavior that he considers immoral; we simply ask if he is hiding a behavior he engaged in. His reaction does not result from a violation of conscience but from fear that his body will trigger fight or flight and he will be detected. For example, we may ask the question: are you concealing any debts. There is no moral component to having debt, it is simply considered unwise and consequently risky to have too much. According to the "conscience" theory no one would ever react to such a question because debt does not violate one's moral code.

Similarly, we could never ask a question about marijuana use of those that believe the law is outdated; those individuals hold that the behavior itself should be legal and of no moral content. Can we effectively test those people on marijuana use? When we ask the question, *are you concealing any marijuana use*, the subject's fight or flight response is triggered not by morality but by fear of detection.

In addition, the fear of detection has nothing to do with conscientious objection to the lying itself. When a lying person is told the examiner will be able to observe his physiological reaction to his concealment, the statement alone almost always enhances the subject's reactivity.

The next question I often hear is, *What about the pathological liar?*

First, there is no such animal—at least as the questioner believes there is. The belief that a person doesn't know he/she is lying because of a psychological condition is simply not true—save psychosis. I often hear this about psychopathy and it is completely untrue. Psychopaths (the clinical term is Anti- Social Personality Disorder) are not separated from reality like psychotics are; they are completely aware of their own deceptions, behavior patterns and lies and hence are as testable as anyone else.

Conversely, a psychotic, by definition, is disconnected to reality. Does this mean that a psychotic can defeat a polygraph? Yes—sometimes. This is NOT a critical issue in the field of polygraph as psychosis is among the most observable of psychological disorders—even by the lay person. Psychotics are often verbally incoherent, delusional and disoriented; it is difficult to NOT recognize them.

In any event, the use of polygraph cannot be concerned with the one in a thousand exception nor can most other technologies. In other words, real life demands we use technologies that are generally reliable but not perfectly so. If we abolish polygraph because it has some degree of imprecision and rely only on the background investigation, we have now moved from a tool with **some** scientific precision to a vehicle with **no** scientific precision i.e. the BI. Does this make sense to anyone?

Polygraph is a diagnostic procedure in that an examiner evaluates the polygraph charts, the narrative of the subject and the behavior of the subject to draw a diagnostic conclusion as to truth, deception or inconclusive. This is similar to what a physician does and medical decisions have their share of inaccuracies.

This is particularly true when doctors use medical imaging devices like the X ray, MRI, Cat Scan etc. A variety of studies examining radiological procedures found that diagnoses were wrong in 20 to 30 percent of cases. [26] Moreover, 10-15 percent of **all** diagnoses are wrong based on autopsy studies. [27] So in the field of medicine, where lives are lost based on an inaccurate diagnosis, we tolerate high levels of error with no calls for abolition of MRIs, X-Rays or cat scans. In the field of polygraph, however, where only jobs and security clearances are on the line, we cannot tolerate any degree of misdiagnoses and consequently all but abolish polygraph in the private sector. And we do this to rely on a tool (the BI) which has no scientific basis! Let me add a personal anecdote illustrating my point.

About three years ago, I developed a vision problem and consulted with an ophthalmologist. She recommended a cat-scan to rule out certain uncommon disorders. About two days after the cat-scan the doctor called me at home—never a good sign. After de-ciphering her "medicalese" she confirmed I had a brain tumor. Needless to say, this was received with a great deal of shock as I listened further to her direction to consult with a neurologist. It took me three very long weeks to get in to see the neurologist who promptly advised that my "condition" was completely benign and required no further treatment, save additional cat-scans every three months. One can only imagine my sense of relief.

---

26 Groopman, J, M.D. *How Doctors Think*, Houghton Mifflin, NY, P181
27 Ibid P 24

As directed, three months later I had another cat-scan done and consulted again with the neurologist. She now advised I had no abnormalities and could discontinue the follow up imaging. I then experienced more relief as I drove away from the doctor's office on cloud nine.

Eventually, I put this all together and realized that what I had experienced was a misdiagnosis. The results of this error resulted in only a great deal of anxiety on my part—certainly nothing of substance compared to the potentialities of this ordeal.

Moreover, my experience was that of a false positive i.e. the perception that something is wrong when it is not. If however a patient receives a false negative, failure to detect a condition that is present, this can result in death. Now THERE is a consequence and I return to my basic point: because cat-scans are sometimes wrong and can result in death, should we ban them? The answer is obvious.

Let me repeat myself—because polygraph and radiology are sometimes wrong is not an argument for abolition. Does anyone argue that medical practice was better before X-Rays, cat scans and MRIs? Would anyone choose to return to those days to eliminate misdiagnoses in radiology and claim we are better off?

Since I am on the topic of misdiagnoses, let me address the point in the polygraph realm. Polygraph charts, like X-Rays, are not as clear as many would hope. It is commonplace to ask three relevant questions and the results are one clear reaction, one clear non-reaction and one partial reaction. This outcome results in a follow up conversation which will, hopefully, further clarify the question and clear the way for specialized testing.

This situation is one of the major reasons we have false positives/false negatives and may well account for much of the existing error rate. In addition, it may also account for much of the resistance to polygraph in that truthful subjects often feel accused when in fact they are truthful.

The follow up conversation mentioned above should not be accusatory other than "accusing" a subject of reactivity to a question. Only after a full cycle of testing is accomplished should the conversation change in tone and would go something like this, "Testing clearly shows that you have not fully discussed your involvement in the issue regarding ……..Clearly there is a reason for that that we have not discussed."

Let me pose a hypothetical case the principle of which is common in polygraph testing.

After a thorough pretest review of the questions to be asked a 65 year old female claims she is completely comfortable with all of the questions-- including crime which was, *Since 18 have you committed an offense for which you could be arrested?* The examinee then reacts consistently to the question. The reactions are not subtle or inconsistent but are clear and convincing. Knowing that 65 year old females rarely commit crimes, the examiner pauses to contemplate the problem and then initiates a conversation with the examinee. This conversation is anything but accusatory but is best described as probing i.e. what might be causing your discomfort on this question? Conversely, examinees almost always interpret the conversation as accusatory implying the subject is hiding some criminal act. After several hours of discussion the examinee eventually admits that her husband was once arrested for Public Lewdness when he was 20 years old. The husband was inebriated at a college football game, removed all his clothes and streaked down the 50 yard line in front of 30,000 mostly laughing football fans. Subject was subsequently arrested, charged and pled guilty to Public Lewdness.

Most of us could look back 30 years and laugh at this behavior treating it like the drunken college prank that it was. This lady, however, is quite religious and was extremely embarrassed by her husband's past behavior. Each time she heard the crime question she flashed back to her husband and consequently reacted strongly to the question.

This reactivity occurred despite the fact that she was fully cognizant that the examiner was asking only about her behavior—no one else's. This kind of misdirected sensitivity happens every day in the polygraph world.

As previously stated we are dealing with the intersection of the mind and the body. This interactivity is usually, but certainly not always, reasonable and rational. Sometimes, despite the fact that we intellectually know something is not relevant and/or significant we nonetheless worry about it. Having forgotten to make the bed, a really neat person may experience stress throughout the day. When he gets home the first thing he does is make the bed. He knows the stress is pointless, even silly, the bed will get made soon enough, but given his psycho-social make up, he cannot help but worry.

In the instant case the 65 year old lady absolutely KNEW her husband's college behavior was outside the thrust of the question but she could not help herself. Once she told the examiner about the issue (2 hours later) she experiences a substantial catharsis and breezed through a follow up test. Had she continued to conceal the reason for her reactivity, she would have failed the polygraph test. The reason she would have failed is that she was, in fact, concealing information on the crime question—but it was not information that the examiner was remotely interested in. Due to her profoundly religious convictions, she had difficulty discussing the issue with the examiner when the examiner repeatedly asked in the pretest, "Now that we have reviewed all the questions is there any reason you would be uncomfortable on any question?"

Had this examinee never come forward with the information about her husband she most certainly would have failed the test. Would that have been a failure of polygraph—or a failure of the examinee to come forward with facilitating information?

This case illustrates one of the many reasons polygraph is unpopular; it quite often necessitates discussion of issues that are embarrassing and sometimes guilt evoking. No one likes to do this i.e. focus on one's own negative behavior and the more undesirable the behavior is the greater the discomfort. This is, I believe, the real reason many oppose use of polygraph.

Another major reason for resistance to polygraph is the fact that a polygraph examiner, without ever uttering the words *lie or liar,* sometimes calls the subject a liar. I hasten to add, this is absolutely verboten; any examiner who actually calls a subject a liar is guilty of malpractice. This should never happen. OK, so we clean this up using phrases like: *You are withholding information, you have a pronounced sensitivity, you haven't told me everything, we haven't discussed the full extent of your involvement in......* In the final analysis, we have made the language less offensive but we really are subtly calling the person a liar. (Even writing these words is counter to all of my own training and makes me shutter.) This is about as offensive as things can get but it is necessary to confront a subject with her own reactions and seek an explanation. This is one of the real reasons for resistance. (Although the culture has undergone rapid change in this venue, up until recently, calling someone a liar was a gross violation of etiquette. This contributed to the **unpopularity** of polygraph.)

I have mentioned that over the years I have fielded hundreds of questions and almost all of them focused on potential false positives. Rarely have people approached me to tell of a case where the brother-in-law was a criminal and passed a poly. The reader may be shocked to learn that lots of people lie in the PS screening process and many of those in the poly process. The post-test discussion sometimes results in disqualifying admissions but just as frequently it helps a subject successfully negotiate the test and obtain a job and/or a security clearance.

Another reason for resistance to the use of polygraph is the notion of invasiveness. The practice of placing sensors on the exterior of the body to obtain patterns from the interior of the body strikes some as invasive—or so they say. Those same people voice no objection to pre-employment physical examinations wherein a physician, often a member of the opposite sex, physically explores one's body cavities. Moreover, science has countermanded the idea that physical examinations produce better health and/or longer lives. Indeed the referenced study notes, *General health checks did not reduce morbidity or mortality, neither overall nor for cardiovascular or cancer causes, although they increased the number of new diagnoses.* Indeed the study further indicates that certain risks are present in physical examinations to wit:

Possible harm from health checks are overdiagnosis, overtreatment, distress or injury from invasive follow-up tests, distress due to false positive test results, false reassurance due to false negative test results, possible continuation of adverse health behaviours due to negative test results, adverse psychosocial effects due to labelling, and difficulties with getting insurance. Last but not least, organised programmes of general health checks are likely to be expensive and may result in lost opportunities to improve other areas of healthcare.[28]

So here again we see that a medical practice which includes exploration of body cavities and has no science to support its validity is somehow not invasive enough to be banned as a pre-employment screening technique but polygraph is. No, placing a few harmless pain free attachments on a person and claiming invasiveness, is not the source of resistance.

I often hear the objection that the scientific imprecision of polygraph testing is grounds for its discontinuance. I have already covered this but want to emphasize the point that few techniques we use for screening,

---

28 Krogsbøll, L, physician, Jørgensen, KJ, physician, Larsen, CJ, physician, Gøtzsche, P. General health checks in adults for reducing morbidity and mortality from disease: Cochrane systematic review and meta-analysis, Nov, 2012, BMJ 2012;345:e7191, Retrieved, 16 Aug 2019, https://www.bmj.com/content/345/bmj.e7191

medical or otherwise, present any scientific precision. Most notably is the HR interview.

HR interviews are an exercise in intuitive guesswork. A number of people talk to a job applicant, sometimes with predetermined script and sometimes not, and make a judgment based on the conversation. The biggest pitfall in this type of interview arises from the familiarity heuristic. This heuristic is exactly what it sounds like i.e. if I find familiarity with an interviewee, for example we determine the subject likes to read the same type of books I do, the unconscious bias of familiarity will affect our judgment. This often happens beyond the scope of awareness and ergo, the bias does not register-- but is nonetheless very real. One searches in vain for credible studies that show "scientific precision" in HR interviews but we still use them. I often wonder why the requirement for scientific precision seems to be applied to polygraph and not many other techniques used in screening.

Other than the polygraph examiner very discreetly implying the subject is lying, I have dismissed all the other so-called objections. So why do so many people strenuously object to poly? It is not because it doesn't work but because it does work.

NOBODY likes to be confronted with poor test results. The only thing worse than a confrontation about an issue that a subject is truthful to is a confrontation regarding an issue a subject is not truthful to. Polygraph is an intrinsically uncomfortable procedure especially if one is untruthful.

We currently live in an extreme populist era where we adore things that make us feel good and abhor things that make us feel bad. Thinking has now taken a distant back seat to feeling and has revived the old statement, "If it feels good, do it." In today's populist world many of our leaders are weak and have tended to rise in response to the highly emotional populism of the day. Few have real principles and are consequently swayed by the mob and its emotional appeals.

In a book that promises to be seminal, Jonathan Haidt and Greg Lukianoff devote an entire chapter to the notion of emotional reasoning defined as letting one's feelings guide interpretation of reality. [29] Ideas are defined as good insofar as they make us feel good and bad insofar as they make us feel bad. We rely too much on our instincts and intuition and not enough on our intellect. This inevitably leads to bad decision making and bad outcomes.

In the early 90s Dow Chemical Company was overwhelmed with lawsuits claiming physical damage to women using Dow's products for breast implants—many of which were needed after mastectomies. The company had to deal with 45 class action suits and formed a 2.3 billion fund for damages. In 1995 Dow declared bankruptcy. Who can deny that women victimized like this by a very large corporation are highly sympathetic people? It was the prefect narrative: women's bodies marred by corporate greed. The story stimulated an uproar of bad feelings toward the company and was largely responsible for the subsequent bankruptcy. [30]

There was, however, one very small problem— the implants did NOT cause any medical issues. This was proven by post-lawsuit scientific analysis by the Mayo clinic; the American Medical Association later concluded that the conversation about the implants were largely hysteria and hype. [31] This is one of many examples of emotional thinking distorting our reality testing—in this case in a big, consequential way. But what, you say, does this have to do with polygraph testing?

The decision to ban polygraph testing via the EPPA was an exercise

---

29 Haidt, J & Lukianoff, G, (2018) *The Coddling of the American Mind*, Penguin Books, NY, P 38.
30 Ropeik, D, How Risky is it, Really? McGraw Hill, NY, P 78 and McKinney, D, *Sen. Warren's Good Work for Dow Chemical*, WSJ editorial, 18 July 2019, P A-13
31 Ibid

in emotional decision making. The decision to not employ screening polygraph in DOD is another such exercise. The FBI refused to use polygraph screening until 2002—after the disastrous Robert Hanssen case.

The bias against polygraph is based not on factual, intellectual analysis but on Haidt and Lukianoff's concept of emotional reasoning—which is really not reasoning at all. Our current age of reliance on feelings is diminishing our tendency to think and analyze and our outcomes show it.

Psychologists call this the Affect Heuristic which is defined as a mental shortcut in decision making which allows for quick and easy problem solving based unconsciously on how much we like someone or something. If the feelings of the decision maker towards an activity are positive, then the judgment that the risks are low and the benefits high is more likely. Conversely, if their feelings towards the activity are unpleasant, they are more likely to perceive the risks as high and benefits low. [32] In simple terms, if we like something we are much more likely to judge it favorably and if we do not like it a negative judgment is more likely. This Affect Heuristic is what stimulates lots of decisions including those pertaining to polygraph.

Throughout this chapter I have made numerous references to polygraph validity and, to this point, have not quoted any research. In 2011-2012 the American Polygraph Association did an exhaustive review of recent polygraph research and found accuracy rates of approximately 80 to 90 percent in a variety of testing techniques.[33] Let me hasten to add

---

32 Finucane, M.L.; Alhakami, A.; Slovic, P.; Johnson, S.M. (January 2000). "The Affect Heuristic in Judgment of Risks and Benefits". Journal of Behavioral Decision Making. 13 (1): 1–17. Retrieved 19 August 2019. https://onlinelibrary.wiley.com/doi/abs/10.1002/%28SICI%291099-0771%2820000103%2913%3A1%3C1%3A%3AAID-BDM333%3E3.0.CO%3B2-S

33 Meta-Analytic Survey of Criterion Accuracy of Validated Polygraph Techniques Polygraph Journal, Special Edition, 2011, 40(4), Report Prepared For The American Polygraph Association Board of Directors Nate Gordon, President (2010-2011) by

that one can find studies that countermand those findings and I refer the reader to the National Academy of Sciences (NAS) commentary on polygraph for an opposing view. Notwithstanding that, there is formidable research supporting the validity and reliability of polygraph. Just what the threshold for "scientific validity" is, the NAS has not said-- nor has anyone else. Is 90% enough for scientific validity? 85%? 80%? That threshold seems to be governed by the Affect Heuristic as well.

My basic point here is that there is a lot of research supporting the validity and reliability of polygraph. My own experience as a researcher suggests that research is flawed insofar as it does not support my own preconceived notions and is superb if it does. (Affect Heuristic again) And, for the last time, use in the real world cannot demand scientific perfection but must have a reasonable degree of valid supporting research.

Cost of polygraph testing varies widely based on the location of the testing—obviously in places like NYC, San Francisco, Los Angeles, Boston etc. it will be more expensive. One reliable website indicates the NYC cost is about $550.00, Philadelphia about $600.00 and Miami about $350.00. The type and length of the test also impacts price. [34]

The reader should note that the cost of background investigations is considerably more than those of polygraph. Of course costs vary based on type and length of the BI but the National Background Investigations Bureau (NBIB) published a cost sheet in 2017 showing the average cost of a BI, both reinvestigation and initials is $1,853.00. [35]

The Ad-Hoc Committee on Validated Techniques, Mike Gougler, Committee Chair, Raymond Nelson, Principal Investigator, Mark Handler, Donald Krapohl, Pam Shaw, Leonard Bierman, Retrieved 19 Aug 2019, https://apoa.memberclicks.net/assets/docs/polygraph_404.pdf

34 Price Capsule, The Cost of Lie Detector Test, Retrieved 21 Aug 2019, https://www.pricecapsule.com/miscellaneous/lie-detector-test-costs.html

35 Phalen, C, Memorandum of 29 March 2017, *FY 2018 Investigations Reimbursable Billing Rates Effective October 1, 2017*, National Background Investigations Bureau, Office of Personnel Management, Retrieved 21 Aug 2019. https://nbib.opm.gov/hr-security-personnel/federal-investigations-notices/2017/fin-17-04.pdf

The reader should also be aware that polygraphs far outstrip BIs for the quality and quantity of information developed. This is both intuitive and true. As I indicated in a previous chapter, the subject interview is, by far, the most productive portion of the BI. The definition of productive used herein refers to the **quantity** of information. This is logical in that no one knows more about the subject than the subject herself.

This same logic is applied to the polygraph but is enhanced by the substantial leverage the poly offers; the mere presence of polygraph may act as a significant deterrent to falsehoods. Moreover, if a subject is less than honest, he may be confronted with this in the post test presenting another opportunity to develop further information for clarification.

In addition to quantity, polygraph tends to collect more substantial information than the BI. For example, on a BI applicants tend to report crimes committed—only if they were identified and apprehended. If they got away with it, we tend to not hear about it. This same dynamic applies to illegal drug use—subjects tend not to report on a BI unless they were arrested. They are usually confident that any potential sources on the BI will NOT report their drug use which, in my 40 years of experience, I have found to be the case. Polygraphs routinely collect information in these areas of drugs and crime when there is no identification or apprehension whereas a BI does not. Moreover, the information collected tends to be more severe than BI information alone. [36]

The author performed background investigations for five years and polygraphs for over 10 years and I can personally attest to enormous volume of data garnered by polygraph. I can safely say that volume substantially exceeds the amount of information collected in the BI—including the subject interview. Once again, this is both intuitive and true.

---

36 Carney, R, PERSEREC, *SSBI Source Yield*, March 1996, PERS-TR-96-001, Retrieved 23 Aug 2019, https://www.dhra.mil/Portals/52/Documents/perserec/tr96-01.pdf

In summary, we see that polygraphs collect a greater volume of information, more substantial information, present a deterrent, cost less and offer the bonus of a statement as to subject's truthfulness or not at the completion of the test. Using the current polygraph lexicon—No Significant Physiological Responses (NSPR) or Significant Physiological Responses (SPR) translates into No Deception Indicated (NDI) or Deception Indicated (DI).

Why did Congress pass a law severely limiting polygraph use in the private sector yet permitted their use in the government sector? Why doesn't every government sector use polygraph to screen employees? The answer is, as I already stated, polygraph is very unpopular and we are now living in a populist world. We need stronger leadership—leadership that is not concerned solely with their own popularity. We also need a population that is less concerned with what feels good (or bad) and can subordinate wants to needs.

CHAPTER FOUR

ADJUDICATIONS

I have already covered the background investigation and the polygraph which are both collection efforts. The obvious question now arises: what do we do with the data collected? How do we determine who is a good risk for hiring or clearing? What rules apply and how do we arrive at those rules?

The Intelligence Community has 13 Adjudicative Guidelines which serve as the underlying core of adjudications. Actually they provide the very basis for PS as a whole in that they elucidate which behaviors are considered and evaluated and which are not. They provide guidance to not only the adjudicator but to the investigator and polygraph examiner as well. These guidelines provide the boundaries of PS processes and include aggravating factors as well as mitigating factors. Despite my previous promise that this book would not be a how to manual, I will list the guidelines here and then discuss. It is important that the reader have some notion of the basic issues in play before we proceed:

Guideline A: Allegiance to the U.S.

Guideline B: Foreign Influence

Guideline C: Foreign Preference

Guideline D: Sexual Behavior

Guideline E: Personal Conduct

Guideline F: Financial Considerations

Guideline G: Alcohol Consumption

Guideline H: Drug Involvement

Guideline I: Psychological Conditions

Guideline J: Criminal Conduct

Guideline K: Handling Protected Information

Guideline L: Outside Activities

Guideline M: Use of Information Technology [37]

Before we launch our discussion, let me provide some history.

Twenty-five years ago, the IC did not have ANY adjudicative guidelines nor did it have any reciprocity. Reciprocity is the acceptance of a security clearance granted by one agency and passed to another agency. If ABC Company has an IT contract with CIA and upon completion is employed by FBI for a similar effort, FBI is supposed to accept that clearance without additional investigation or adjudication. That is the way the IC is supposed to work today and does—to some extent. It was not always thus.

---

[37] Center for the Development of Security Excellence, DoD Security Specialist Course: Personnel Security, April, 2015, P 1, Retrieved 23 Aug, 2019. https://www.cdse.edu/documents/cdse/job-aid-13-adjudicative-guidelines-v2.pdf

Before reciprocity, FBI started the investigative process all over again before they could contract with ABC Company. This process can take anywhere from 6 to 18 months and entails significant costs. The practice emanated from the "stovepiping" so common to the federal government 30 years ago. As the 911 Commission so aptly pointed out, government agencies, notably CIA and FBI, did not appropriately share intelligence. This non-sharing was born of "The Wall" intentionally erected by Congress between the two agencies ostensibly to preserve civil liberties. [38] The idea of a secret organization like CIA providing overseas intelligence, sometimes on U.S. citizens, to the FBI was/is a daunting idea. This fear fed the notion of need to know and non-sharing in general. It is also undeniably true that CIA and FBI had a long standing rivalry that reinforced this instinct to not share.

The notion of non-reciprocity flourished in this environment; indeed it seemed to be the natural way to do business. It is important to note, however, that the IC was working on reciprocity well before 911 and the work continues today. 911, however, gave it an enormous boost.

As part of the drive toward reciprocity, common standards were adopted by the IC. The design was if agencies used the same standards then reciprocity should be greatly facilitated. That is the reason we have adjudicative guidelines used throughout the IC today. They serve as the bedrock of the security clearance process and provide commonality of design and some semblance of consistency in outcomes.

At the risk of digressing too much, it is important to define the term *consistency*. Consistency does NOT mean sameness. The guidelines are written to promote similarity, particularly in outcomes but this does not mean that different agencies must implement the guidelines exactly the same.

For example, Guideline H dealing with drug usage states that RECENT

---

38 911 Commission Report, Norton & Co, NYC, P 417

drug use can be disqualifying. What is the definition of recent? There is none and this is not a lapse, it is by design.

It is entirely reasonable that the Drug Enforcement Administration (DEA) may want to enforce a stricter standard on past drug use than the State Department. This can easily speak to the agency's credibility; who wants a DEA agent testifying on the stand in a courtroom with recent drug use in his own past? Similarly, the Treasury Department may want to be more strident in adjudicating financial matters.

The adjudicative guidelines, like any policy, define the outer boundaries of activities and leave the middling behavior to the implementer's best judgment. That is the definition of good policy. It cannot be too restrictive. It must provide, however, some limits while at the same time allowing for enough flexibility to get the job done. We certainly should not shrink from the notion of a State Department employee using marijuana once or twice in the year before employment while the same behavior evokes a disqualification at DEA or FBI. Consistency does not demand sameness and reasonable flexibility is necessary to function in the real world.

For example, the guideline on sexual behavior allows for pursuit of criminal sexual behavior and/or paraphilias, but specifically forbids consideration of sexual orientation. This is exactly what policy is supposed to do i.e. describe what is acceptable and what is not acceptable thereby eliminating extremes but leaving a reasonable midfield for evaluation.

I hear too many people in the IC who demand sameness. "This guy got a clearance having used marijuana twice in the last year but this guy got disqualified with the same behavior." This brings me to one of the core issues in PS, that of the Whole Person Concept.

The Whole Person Concept is exactly what it sounds like—when adjudicating we consider every available aspect of the subject's existence, to include the good and the bad. Each adjudicative guideline includes potentially disqualifying factors as well as mitigating factors. Many cases have some mix of the two and it is up to the adjudicator to balance the two and make a reasonable judgment.

Continuing on with the example of illegal drug use, recency is a prime mitigating factor (in this as well as most other behaviors.) Let's assume we have a twenty five year old, single male who graduated from college three years ago. The only derogatory information developed during the investigation was his use of marijuana once a week for four years while in college. Since graduation from college the subject has not used any illegal drugs. He volunteered this information during the subject interview and it was confirmed by a source who was his college roommate.

The three years of abstinence is a strong mitigating factor alone. His behavior changed with a significant change in environment i.e. he graduated from college and was no longer living in an environment where the drug was constantly present. This is a credible reason for abstinence and he volunteered the information giving him additional credibility. This honesty suggests some character and integrity and adds credence to whatever other statements he has made throughout the process. As always, however, his honesty is not THE deciding factor but one indicator among many that must be considered in the final adjudication. The three year period of abstinence combined with his forthrightness both act as mitigating factors. Based on my own 40 years of experience, recency is the most frequently applied mitigating factor but there are two sides to this coin.

While recency is thought to be a reasonable indicator of future behavior, there is something called *recency bias* defined as the tendency to think that trends and patterns we observe in the recent past will continue in the future. [39] That is-- an **over-reliance** on recency may result in a biased judgment. We do tend to sometimes over-rely on recent data because it is more prominent in the mind/psyche. It is hard not to do this. Having said this, however, it is important to note that any over-reliance on a single indicator is unwise and may result in poor decisions.

If the above statements appear to be contradictory (recency is an excellent behavioral indicator vs. recency bias) that is because the world of human behavior is exceedingly complicated. The most realistic statement adjudicators can rely on is that recency is USUALLY an indicator of future behavior but not always. This is a perfect example of why we need adjudicators who are skilled, intelligent and well informed. They also need to be willing to face risk and sometimes be proven wrong.

This something the culture does not welcome—being wrong. In our rush to hold everyone accountable for their actions (a healthy inclination overall) we often forget that anyone who makes decisions will occasionally be wrong. This goes for bond traders, doctors, lawyers, high level executives and adjudicators. It is a concept that is rapidly diminishing and makes most of us risk averse. My own experience with two large bureaucracies (NYPD and CIA) certainly reaffirms this notion and suggests success is largely the absence of mistakes. This is, of course, completely denied by the heads of the bureaucracies but is nonetheless true. This was not always the case.

In the late 50s, after the Soviet Union launched Sputnick, the U.S. went into near panic mode. Our science was clearly behind theirs and space activity suggested a whole new avenue of warfare and hence vulnerability. Our attempts to launch a satellite resulted in 12 failures followed by our first success. This was clearly driven by fear and no one was

---

39 Carroll RT, (1994) The Skeptic's Dictionary, Retrieved, 25 Aug, 2019, http://www.skepdic.com/recencybias.html

held "accountable." True science recognizes that failure is part of the path to success.

Similar to our experience almost 60 years ago, Iran has experienced three launch failures in their quest to launch a satellite. [40] No doubt it is only a matter of time before they succeed. Virtually all other countries who have space programs have also encountered failure. Such events are not unique to U.S. history.

Today, however, 12 failures would not be tolerated. Heads would roll and whichever "head" was at the tail end and met success by virtue of timing would be hailed as a hero. Moreover, those failures dealt in the hard sciences; areas that lent themselves to reliable, formulaic calculations. The world of Personnel Security is a subset of social sciences dealing with human behavior and thus intrinsically more difficult to navigate.

Personnel Security is a field fraught with risk; if one stays in the field long enough one will encounter being wrong. The only way to never be wrong is to deny everyone a clearance or a job. That is not an option but many of us tilt in that direction due to risk aversion.

In addition to recency it is fairly obvious that the gravity of a behavior is of equal weight in making adjudicative decisions. Gravity is determined by a common sense evaluation of a particular behavior. Shoplifting a $5.00 item and bank robbery totaling $50,000 are both thefts but the latter is certainly more substantial and of greater concern.

The above example is obvious for illustrative reasons—no one would equate bank robbery to shoplifting. The real world, however, is rarely so clear and an adjudicator is more likely to evaluate shoplifting a $10.00 item versus theft of $10.00 worth of office equipment from an employer. This is the reason we have judges and adjudicators—not

---

40 Associated Press, Washington Times, P A-8, 30 August 2019, No author.

to just read laws and guidelines but to evaluate behavior in its fullest context.

Similarly, frequency of a behavior is also vital to the whole person concept. The greater the frequency the greater the impact is on an adjudicative outcome. Smoking marijuana once is almost never a concern and smoking it every day is almost always a concern.

This speaks to a **pattern** of behavior; behaviors displayed consistently over a longer period are much more likely to suggest future behavior. Habits are, by definition, recurring activities and are considerably more difficult to change. If a subject of investigation consistently engages in an untoward activity this suggests a psychological investment in the behavior and a greater predisposition to continuity.

Consideration of any behavioral aspects, but especially gravity of conduct must be evaluated in accordance with one of the bedrock principles of PS—context and proportionality. It is impossible to properly evaluate conduct without a full understanding of the context of the act. Situational factors can commonly change the moral and/or social implications of activities. Let us return to a prior example.

A 20 year old male attending college gets thoroughly inebriated at a campus football game. At some point during the game he removes all his clothes and streaks down the fifty yard line in front of thousands of fans. He is promptly arrested for Public Lewdness, charged and pleads guilty at arraignment. He is given a fine, 30 days of community service and a brief period of probation. Now, Public Lewdness more often than not, constitutes exhibitionism which usually refers to a male displaying his genitalia to an un-consenting female. Absent context of the act most of us would conclude the conduct was criminal and egregious-- not to mention disqualifying. The context, however, redefines the behavior as prankish and probably thoroughly acceptable in adjudication.

Similarly, proportionality essentially addresses the question of—how much, how bad? Not all unacceptable acts, even very similar acts, are equally so; some clearly are worse than others. Let me provide another example, this time a real world example from the aforementioned Edward Howard case. I mentioned Howard committed a theft but did not provide the context.

On a long flight, Howard had a few drinks and struck up a friendly conversation with the woman sitting next to him. They chatted for hours and seemed to really enjoy each other's company. Upon exiting the flight, Howard claimed the woman forgot her purse and he removed a small amount of cash, somewhere in the neighborhood of $20.00. [41] He self-reported this information to David Wise who spent a great deal of time with Howard interviewing him for a book. We will accept this version of events despite the dubiousness of a woman "forgetting" her purse on a plane full of strangers.

This theft was **personal.** He stole this money directly from a person he had interacted with and apparently liked. Given the act was personal, the fact that the amount was relatively small is NOT mitigating.

Similarly if I invite you to my house for a party and you find a twenty dollar bill in the restroom and keep it, you have committed a kind of personal theft.

Let's contrast this with a twenty dollar theft on your income tax return of $700.00. You exaggerated your charitable deductions to squeeze out another $20.00 to rise to $700.00 rather than 680.00. You advise your adjudicator of the income tax theft. Are all three of these thefts the same? Does not context and proportionality define them differently?

(I cannot resist adding this personal anecdote. I once asked my wife,

---

41 Wise, P 131

an ex-nun, if she would get me a Xerox copy of a personal three page document at her workplace, the CIA. She was uncomfortable with this request—about which I laughed out loud!)

The real adjudicative question deals with this: Is the theft a reflection of an overall lack of honesty and integrity or is it a minor transgression stating little to nothing significant about the person's character? Do the circumstances of the theft really define it or all $20.00 thefts, whether from the federal government or your close friend the same? I think the former but some would disagree.

In the world of adjudications we have hawks and doves. It is important for the reader to know that real adjudicative decisions, that is, on close call cases with derogatory or noteworthy information, the final call is made by a high level official after substantial review. Typically, a lower level employee will make the initial recommendation and a number of senior officials will weigh in up the line. Nonetheless the higher level official may well be a hawk or a dove herself.

In the Intelligence Community we have made a strenuous effort to be consistent—although consistency is not sameness. We do NOT feel compelled to have every case with 2x marijuana use in the past year come out with the same outcome--denial. What we strive for is reasonability. If one person is denied for two time marijuana use another might not be because their use was more reasonable. For example, one person may have legitimately used medical marijuana for treatment of nausea after chemotherapy. This was done after other anti-nausea drugs were tried and were ineffective. Who would deny a clearance or a job to this person?

This urge for consistency emanates largely from an innate and admirable sense of fairness and equality. A sense of fairness seems to be inherent in humans and is the source of much progress throughout the ages. Outcomes of various actions, however, are not equal and, in some cases, they should not be.

The PS process eliminates many more men for criminal activity-- as compared to women. Since men and women are roughly 50% of the population shouldn't our jails be 50% men and 50% women?

Men are about 93% of our federal prison population and women only 7%. Does this prove brazen unfairness and inequality of treatment? Does this show that the Personnel Security screening system is blatantly unfair because more men than women are disapproved on the issue of crime? Does this unequal outcome need to be addressed and systemic changes made?

The obvious reason is that men commit more crime than women at a rate of about 3 to 1. In the area of violent crime (which accounts for most incarceration) the differential is about 4 to 1. [42] As a society we are consumed with never admitting that there are gender differences either inherent or behavioral. The crime data appears to disprove that notion and is reflected in PS outcomes. The point here is that unequal outcomes, like denying males a job because of past crime more frequently, do not ALWAYS indicate unfairness.

In any event, when dealing with human behavior in an adjudicative framework, no two cases are exactly alike. There are always nuances that differ and make one case slightly different from the next. The effort in the IC is to minimize subjectivity and differences in outcomes while recognizing there is no way to perfectly accomplish that. Companies adopting a PS system need to recognize that as well.

In discussing adjudications it is important to note that there are two types: One for prospective employees and another for existing employees. The difference between the two is enormous. In the case of

---

[42] FBI Uniform Crime Reporting Statistics, 2015, Crime in the United States, 2015, Retrieved 4 Sept 2019, https://ucr.fbi.gov/crime-in-the-u.s/2015/crime-in-the-u.s.-2015/tables/table-42

a prospective employee an adjudicator may, in effect, deny a person a job that he did not have in the first place. This may be very unpleasant but it is not life changing. Conversely, in dealing with a long time employee who is uncovered engaging in some objectionable behavior, an unfavorable adjudication may threaten her existing livelihood. This is obviously of much greater impact than the denial of a job one never had-- and ergo must be adjudicated accordingly. Frankly, the long term employee must be given greater leeway because losing one's job is almost always a traumatic experience often resulting in an extreme behavioral response. (See the Howard case above) Moreover, in terminating someone we may also be affecting the individual's family. Houses may need to be sold, children uprooted from schools, long established roles of spouses reversed etc. For these reasons adjudicators must be **extremely** judicious in evaluating reinvestigation cases.

To this point I have discussed adjudications as a bipolar choice i.e. Approve or deny. Fortunately in the case of reinvestigations we may have additional options short of termination to include suspension, probation, reimbursement of misappropriated funds to the company, reduction in title or rank, fines, salary reduction and/or transfer.

In the event termination is necessary, experience has taught us that a soft landing is always a wise alternative. Severance pay, transition pay, counseling, legal advice, assistance in obtaining new employment and temporary extension of health insurance all can help to ease the blow and make the transition adjustment more palatable. Why, you ask, should we provide this rather extensive support to someone who undoubtedly engaged in egregious behavior resulting in termination? Shouldn't we let him get what he apparently deserves?

This leads me to a very important issue—at least in the national security venue. In adjudicating cases we are not in the business of making **moral** judgments; we are in the business of making judgments as to the risk to national security.

It may be true that John Smith cannot manage his finances and consequently is in chronic debt. This issue has no moral component to it—it is not morally wrong to run up burdensome debt and it is not illegal to do so. It is, however, unwise to do so and may display a vulnerability and evidence of a lack of self-restraint.

Allstate Insurance Company did a review of 60,000 policyholders and found that these with substantial credit problems cost the company 40% more in claims.[43] Money management skills are an important life skill and in many cases may well be reflective of overall self-discipline.

Let me further illustrate with an example that relies on moral behavior but nonetheless does not constitute a moral judgment. Using my prior example of theft, it is certainly true that stealing is immoral; it is recognized as such in all cultures. Not all stealing is equally immoral, however. Most of us view stealing from a widow with children as worse than stealing from a rich corporation. The impact is grave in the former and almost non-existent in the latter. Stealing from a widow may be immoral but from a PS perspective, it informs us that this person is not trustworthy and hence why would we trust him with national security information? Ergo we have made an amoral judgment based on immoral behavior. The two are most often in accord but our focus is on the statement a behavior makes as to trustworthiness.

The background investigation and polygraph are information collecting modalities while adjudicative elements determine how to evaluate the data gathered and make the ultimate decision to grant and/or hire. While we strive for consistency we must not mistake sameness for consistency and remain flexible enough to make intelligent, case by case decisions. Given the complicated nature and nuances of human behavior the adjudication phase may be considered the most challenging aspect of Personnel Security.

---

43 Boundy, D. (1993). When money is the drug, The compulsion for credit cash and chronic debt. NY: Harper Collins

CHAPTER FIVE

PSYCHOLOGY AND PERSONNEL SECURITY

Since Personnel Security deals with human behavior it is obvious that the mental health professional should have some role in the process. While most frequently we look at past behavior to project future behavior, often that past behavior is more complicated and evaluation of it may be enhanced by a clinical perspective. In an ideal world all PS units would have real time access to a mental health professional but that is not always the case. Obviously this chapter cannot be a Psychology 101 course so I will attend to the psychological tenets/issues that I have found to be most germane to PS.

I would like to begin this discussion with the issue of cognitive biases which seriously impact our decision-making—and often not for the better. This is critically important when considering the adjudication factor in that our decisions are often unconsciously colored by these biases. We may have no idea of the inherent presence of these psychic influences and ergo they may become dominant and highly toxic. There is a long list of these psychological predispositions but I will focus only on those that are most prevalent.

Perhaps the most common and impacting cognitive bias is confirmation bias. This is the instinct to unconsciously search for information supporting our preconceived notion and, when we find it, automatically assume our position is right. "Right" in this case is equates to the perception of accuracy and/or a moral appropriateness.

This bias emanates from our wish/need to be right which is undergirded by Leon Festinger's concept of Cognitive Dissonance. This is defined as conflict resulting from a behavioral or ideational violation of our own code –I smoke but I know it is bad for my health. We typically deal with this in one of four ways: Change the behavior, rationalize the issue, justify the behavior/cognition by adding another behavior or denial. [44]

Confirmation bias may be the easiest trap to fall into because it feels so good. Being right elevates our mood and provides a feeling of warmth and comfort. It also negates further effort—why do I need to do any more work on this project since I now know I have the right position? In a word, confirmation bias is EASY and easy has a very large psychological constituency.

Another significant and common bias is the availability heuristic. We tend to rely on immediate examples that readily come to mind when evaluating an issue. This bias operates on the notion that something quickly and effortlessly recalled must be important and outweighs other unrecalled issues. [45] This too is easy and is thus self-re-enforcing. Travel to Israel often conjures images of terrorist activity but rarely of automobile accidents because the former is frequently portrayed in the media but the latter almost never. Hence we may conclude that terrorist threats in Israel present a greater danger than accidents—which is clearly not the case.

---

44 Festinger, L. (1957) *A Theory of Cognitive Dissonance*, Stanford University Press, Ca.
45 Esgate, A. Groome, D. (2005).
An Introduction to Applied Cognitive Psychology. Psychology Press. p. 201.

Affect bias can also negatively impact our decision making. Affect bias is the implicit, and often unconscious, placement of value (good or bad) on a person, place or thing.[46] Once unconsciously labeled "good" the activity is much more likely to be favorably received by the individual. This tendency is often referred to as, "Going with the gut" or instinctive decision making. We tend to like this because, when we are right, it feels good. It especially makes us feel good because, once again, it is easy. We need not invest any labor in tedious research which may or may not clarify the situation, hence the power of this bias is compounded. Stated in laymen's terms, if we like something/somebody we are much more prone to accept it/them whereas if we dislike them we are more prone to rejection. I would wager the reader has seen this bias in the workplace —and probably more than once. People who are popular, as opposed to hard working, industrious and efficient, tend to get treated better at work. The affect bias is the primary reason this unfortunate state of affairs so often exists.

The optimism bias is the belief that we will suffer less trials and tribulations in life and that we will have far greater success than average.[47] This bias is two- fold; it can cause us to make foolish decisions like engaging in risky behaviors because we are less likely to experience untoward outcomes or it provides a positive sense of anticipation about the future. The latter propels us forward to experiment and to pursue goals and objectives. In the absence of the optimism bias who would start college knowing/thinking they would fail? Who would take a trip to an unknown place? A sense of optimism informs us that college and the trip will be positive. Similarly, most of us believe that cancer will not happen to us but to the other guy. What would life be like if we woke up every day worrying about cancer? In that sense, the optimism

---

46 Cherry, K, *The Affect Heuristic and Decision Making,* verywell mind, 13 Aug 2019, retrieved 9 Sept 2019, https://www.verywellmind.com/what-is-the-affect-heuristic-2795028

47 Cherry, *Understanding the Optimism Bias AKA the Illusion of Invulnerability* 12 Aug, 2019, Retrieved 10 Sept, 2019, https://www.verywellmind.com/what-is-the-optimism-bias-2795031

bias provides a remedy from excessive, regular anxiety and supports a path forward to success.

From a PS perspective, the optimism bias can lead to faulty assumptions about future behavior. We may decide to take risks on individuals that are not warranted by the facts of the case. Our "superior" ability to make decisions may lead to unfavorable outcomes. This can be particularly true when dealing with infrequent events; if an adjudicator believes that mass shootings are rare (and they are) he/she is more likely to assume risk in cases suggestive of violence. For example, if a person has been convicted of domestic violence, served his time and vocalizes contrition these mitigating factors may take on more import than they should. The adjudicator's unwarranted optimism in his own ability may drive him toward approval.

The last bias I will cover is the familiarity bias which is the tendency to favor a person who is like us. Let's say an applicant is from the same small home town as us and went to the same high school as us. We are more likely to favorably receive this individual than another who is completely foreign to us. Investors are more likely to invest in securities that they are familiar with than those they are not.[48] PS professionals, like everyone else, are afflicted with this bias. The best method of handling this bias is to pass off the case to another person to handle. It is very difficult to handle cases we are familiar with without this bias tainting our judgment.

There are many other common cognitive biases but the list is too long to discuss all of them. The very large question of what do we do about these biases looms large in any organization.

There is a "treatment" for cognitive biases called Cognitive Bias Modification (CBM) which focuses largely on psychological deficits and

---

[48] Nofsinger, J. Ph.D. *Familiarity Bias PART I: What is it?* Psychology Today, 25 July 2008, retrieved 10 Sept, 2019, https://www.psychologytoday.com/intl/blog/mind-my-money/200807/familiarity-bias-part-i-what-is-it

attempts to redirect our psychic focus away from negative attention-related issues. For example, our inner psychic forces may unknowingly drive us to focus too much on peer achievements-- to the detriment of our self-esteem. This is consistent with basic Freudian technique i.e. drawing psychic issues from the unconscious to the conscious so that we can deal with them. This treatment is not relevant for our purposes but suffice to say that calling attention to our unconscious biases goes a long way toward minimizing or eradicating them.

Indeed, consciousness-raising regarding cognitive biases is often sufficient enough alone to equip us to overcome them. Since they dwell mostly in the unconscious, removal from unawareness shifts us to the cognitive level where we can "reason" with our biases. Any PS training program should include a segment on cognitive biases and, having done this myself, I can almost guarantee, it will be well received and generate significant returns.

The PS professional will likely encounter some mental health issues in her career. Among the most common disorders we see in the PS field are: Depressive disorders, Anti-Social Personality Disorder (Psychopathy) and Narcissism.

Suffice to say here that the PS professional needs to be somewhat familiar with these disorders and, if at all possible, the PS program should have a mental health professional available for consultation. Only a clinician can make a diagnosis of a PS subject and only after meeting face to face with the subject. More often, however, the PS officer will deal with someone who falls short of diagnosable but instead has traits similar to the disorder. The latter may not **require** a clinician but it is preferable.

Many larger government agencies involved in national security employ psychological testing as a part of the screening protocol. Psychological testing is the administration of psychological tests, which are supposed to be an objective and standardized measure of a sample of behavior.[49] Among the two most commonly used instruments are the Mental Status Examination (MSE) and the Minnesota Multiphasic Personality Inventory (MMPI)

The MSE is a structured observation/interaction by a mental health professional focusing on the domains of judgment, appearance, attitude, behavior, and affect, speech, thought process, thought content, cognition, perception, insight, and mood.[50] The MMPI (the most widely used) is a true false questionnaire administered as a part of an overall clinical assessment designed to identify abnormal behavior. It includes a validity testing element to determine if the subject is honest and truthful.[51] Both are believed by mental health professionals to be largely valid i.e. they measure what they are supposed to measure and do so consistently, and reliable –they consistently produce replicable outcomes.

These instruments should not be used rigidly and inflexibly in a PS screening program. Often the clinician will use the outcomes to further explore areas of concern manifested by the test and come to a holistic judgment. It is not used and should not be used as a threshold of acceptance or rejection i.e. subject scored X so she is eliminated.

These testing modalities are very expensive and consequently a company may want to use them only for high risk and/or high influence positions. Perhaps a "mere" clinical interview can be employed at less cost and still make a contribution to the process. As I emphasized in my discussion of polygraph, these processes are not scientifically perfect but when used appropriately can enhance the screening process.

---

49 Urbina, S & Anastasi, A. (1997). *Psychological testing* (7th ed.) Upper Saddle River, NJ: Prentice Hall. p.4.
50 Trzepacz, PT & Baker RW (1993). *The Psychiatric Mental Status Examination*. Oxford, U.K.: Oxford University Press. p. 202.
51 Framingham, J, Ph.D. *The Minnesota Multiphasic Personality Inventory (MMPI)* Psych Central, Retrieved 12 Sept 2019, https://psychcentral.com/lib/minnesota-multiphasic-personality-inventory-mmpi/

As aforementioned, I am describing the Rolls Royce model of a PS program; it is up to the company/agency to decide what is affordable and produces proportionate returns.

One of the reasons psychological testing can be useful is that it may minimize potential subjectivity in the PS process. One prime example of this can be seen in the management of the sympathetic subject.

A sympathetic subject is exactly what it sounds like—an individual who evokes positive emotions. This is someone we like even if we never met her but her past experience, in one vein, is appealing to us. A typical sympathetic subject might be a person who works her way through college via a part time job and student loans. At graduation she may owe $50,000. Immediately we empathize with this person and unconsciously "root" for her successful completion of the PS vetting process. I might call this the sympathy bias but in the real world it is called the affect heuristic. This feeling may be unavoidable but the PS professional must be very cautious that it does not impact his judgment.

As a young polygraph examiner we were taught to NOT to be overly friendly with our testing subjects; to do so is to risk sympathy bias and develop a liking of our subject. I initially disdained this and tried hard to be warm and friendly to all subjects. I reasoned that doing so would develop rapport—a necessary ingredient in an examiner/examinee relationship. I soon discovered that to have an objective, post-test discussion about some possible prevarication was much more difficult if I allowed myself to like the examinee. In short, I was unconsciously and unintentionally "siding" with the subject when he needed frank and objective straight talk. I quickly learned the wisdom of my instructors and thereafter retained a professional distance. In the final analysis, I did a better job because I had little to no feelings for my subject. I was in a better position to, at times, confront the subject with his own test shortcomings.

Sometimes this "confrontation" was really just a conversation and those conversations require genuine skill and dexterity to discern the truth. It also involved understanding the psychology of interviewing and sometimes the psychology of interrogation. The skill of interviewing is the most basic tool in the arsenal of the PS profession ergo I will spend significant time discussing the psychology of interviewing and interrogation.

Now *interrogation* is a bad word which conjures up all kinds of bad images and ergo requires a true definition. Interrogation is the conversational effort to overcome an interrogation subject's resistance to telling the truth. Information elicitation is the mere collection of details with no resistance from the subject. [52] It is often the case that a PS professional interviews/interrogates an individual and when the subject agrees to provide information the interviewer then shifts gears and gathers the details germane to the issue. This raises the obvious question: Why do some subjects resist and others disclose?

As a prefacing comment, there are two types of interviews—a custodial interview and a non-custodial session. The definition is exactly what it sounds like, to wit, in the custodial interview the subject may NOT leave and in the non-custodial modality she can leave anytime she wants. PS interviews are almost always of the latter type. No one can legally force anyone to undergo PS processing but, obviously, if one chooses to not undergo, or terminates PS processing the goal the subject is seeking (a job or a clearance) is lost. This is a very important distinction. I will limit my discussion to non-custodial interviewing/interrogation and start with the question, *why do non-custodial interview subjects resist telling the truth?* There are a plethora of psycho-social constructs that support resistance; I will offer a few of the most pronounced.

At the risk of insulting the reader with the obvious, perhaps the most

---

52 Thiessen, M, (2010) *Courting Disaster*, Regnery Publishing, NY, NY

prevalent reason for resistance is fear of consequences. A subject may have considered her behavior and made a decision that, if admitted, the behavior would disqualify her from consideration. To make this decision intelligently, a subject must have solid knowledge of behavioral requirements. They rarely have such knowledge especially in initial applications. They may have an accurate, generic idea i.e. the FBI will deny me for excessive drug use but what constitutes that definition is rarely known or understood. Even in reinvestigation cases where a subject has been an employee and is familiar with the rules and regulations, they are, more often than not, wrong in their knowledge and interpretation of the rules.

This is an important point for the interviewer. While the interviewer must be REALLY careful not to misrepresent the facts, he must explain the issue in psychological terms of transparence and frame it in such a way that revealing the truth will be more promising than continuing to conceal it. Certainly, it is the case that often a subject is accurate in his assumption of disqualifying wrongdoing but, just as often, that is not the case and his assessment is wrong. So a cognitive reframing may be a good interview approach to the subject who, the interviewer senses, is concealing information. To offer an example from the polygraph world, "Joe, you failed to complete the test based on your past drug use. At this point, we cannot proceed further and hence you have nothing to lose by offering a fuller definition of that usage."

The emotions of embarrassment, guilt and shame also drive people to conceal information. Embarrassment is the least of these emotions and may have no relationship to morality. A behavior may not be morally wrong yet we can still be thoroughly embarrassed by it and wish to hide it. In discussing possible substance abuse, a single 40 year old female may be incredibly embarrassed by her getting very drunk and then having sex with a single 22 year old male-- despite the fact that no laws or regulations were violated.

Guilt is quite different in that it almost always has a moral dimension. The wish to hide the activity may be intensified if the act was ego syntonic i.e. it is in accord with one's own code of conduct as compared to ego dystonic, it violates one's own ethics. This differentiation is important to the interviewer because the former is almost always much more difficult to draw out from a reluctant subject. Let's assume you agree with strict DUI laws but disagree with an extreme definition of DUI. If you get arrested in one state with a .04 level of alcohol you may be less reluctant to admit the offense as compared to an arrest for a .10 level. The .04 arrest does not violate your own code but the .10 arrest does-- hence the latter is more difficult to admit.

Shame is the most difficult emotion to handle in an interview because it is the most intense and deep-seated. I dare say the majority of child molesters are deeply ashamed of their urges and actions and hence take extreme measures to hide those ideas and actions. An interviewer needs to try to remove/minimize the shame factor from the conversation and try to make the subject more comfortable in making an admission—a tall task indeed in the case of pedophilia.

Fear of failure, particularly for mid-life males, can be an overriding reason for withholding information. Male fear of failure resides in bowels of the male psyche and drives behavior more than we care to admit. In a post arrest interview, the spy Aldridge Ames was asked why he did it and he replied,

…having the money became more important not for what I could buy with it but because of what it said about me. What did it say about you? It said Rick Ames was not a failure.[53]

Information about past wrongdoing can represent failure for an interviewee and, as such, may be difficult to discuss. The interviewer should reframe the experience, to the extent he can speculate what it is, as a

---

[53] Earley, P. (1997) Confessions of a Spy, Putnam & Sons, NY, P 252

non-failure and a mere human capitulation to vulnerability. Sometimes this can be a hard sell and other times an easy sell; the subject often wants to believe the act was only a mistake that could have been made by anyone. This represents the easy sell while the hard sell may be a truly egregious event that subject is profoundly ashamed of. The latter are among the most difficult of admissions to obtain.

One final psychosocial construct supporting resistance may be the subject's own psychological investment in his denial. The more a subject is able to deny his activity the more hardened he may become in that denial and the more difficult it may become to reverse his position and save face. The reader should think about the last time he/she had a trivial discussion about some unimportant issue with someone disagreeing with him/her and how, as the discussion proceeded, you became more entrenched in your position. This is a near-universal psychic tendency. For this reason the interviewer should disallow denials with both verbal and non-verbal commands.

There are many other reasons for resistance but these are among the most prevalent. Let me now turn to the psychological constructs supporting truth- telling.

One powerful psychosocial force in truth telling can be a desire for moral justification. Other than hard core psychopaths, most of us seek moral approval and will often go to some lengths to attain it. If the interviewer implies that such approval will be forthcoming upon disclosure of the behavior, this can be a powerful force propelling an interviewee toward the truth. This is particularly so in cases of more serious wrongdoing which does lend itself to quick and easy rationalization. The interviewer needs to be careful not to state outright that the behavior is morally acceptable but rather should speak to the underlying conflict the subject may be struggling with. For example, in a rape case, the interviewer might state that he understands the strength of the sex drive coupled with an urge for revenge against women (or a woman) and can readily see how the subject fell prone to those dynamics. This technique can be successful in non-custodial cases with interviewees who are NOT hard core criminals but rarely works with lifetime criminals.

Another potential force for honesty can be the inevitability of solid evidence. The subject may be engaging in risk/benefit thinking when deciding whether to volunteer inculpatory information. In these cases the determination to provide information is more intellectual than psychological; the subject makes a conscious choice because she sees that she is trapped by evidence and can perhaps ameliorate the situation with new information. For example, "Jane, we have the vouchers of your last five trips and we have checked the hotel rates you submitted with those of the hotel archives. You clearly overcharged." Essentially the subject decides she is caught and there is no point in further resistance.

Another psychological force supporting truthfulness is the desire for approval. I have been amazed over the years in the number of subjects who, when confronted by a stranger, have a strong urge to obtain the stranger's approval. This makes no sense; the subject may know he will never see the interviewer again but in the span of the interview, he nonetheless seeks the approval of the interviewer. From the perspective of evolutionary psychology this may date back to prehistoric times when approval of the tribe could literally mean life or death. An outcast from the tribe usually died from any number of causes and consequently the desire for approval may be organically implanted in our brains.

This can be compounded by another psychic instinct-- the affect heuristic. If the subject likes the interviewer his wish for acceptance/approval may be intensified. Conversely, if the subject dislikes the interviewer there is almost zero chance of gaining new information. The affect heuristic in reverse tends to eliminate any chance the subject will admit anything. The reader should ask herself—would I volunteer incriminating information to someone I dislike and/or I believe to be obnoxious and incompetent?

Another construct supporting truth telling is what I call the immediacy heuristic. This notion tells us that what is immediately before us, as compared to months or years down the road, has much more potential to impact our behavior now. How is this relevant to interviewing?

We can capitalize on the immediacy heuristic by employing the psychological phenomenon of catharsis. Catharsis is the physiological relief that one experiences upon deciding to tell the truth after lying. One actually feels measurably and perceptibly better after a truthful admission. This is consistently and accurately measured on a polygraph. In all likelihood, the reader has actually experienced this phenomenon at one time or another.

In an interviewing context, the interviewer can promise that the subject will feel better RIGHT NOW if he tells the truth. There need not be any mention of reward (a job or clearance) down the road; the reward is the feeling of relief that will occur immediately at the time of admission. This reward also has the additional positive quality of being utterly simple and lacking the usual complexity of the behavior/reward cycle. It can be much more powerful than the statement—*Study for four years in college and you will get a better job in 2023*. The promise of a better job in 2023 is almost always true but separated by lots of work and four years. For an interviewer to be able to offer an **immediate** reward for honesty is indeed powerful.

Appeals to ego can also have a truth inducing effect. This can be effectively coupled with evidence countermanding the subject's narrative. In pointing out the shortcomings of a person's narrative and appealing to their native intelligence (ego) an interviewer may make the subject feel unworthy of his own description of events and the truth may come out as an ego-saving tactic. Statements like, "Mary, surely you can see the numerous inconsistencies in your narrative and you are now in a position to correct those inconsistencies" can be quite productive.

There are many other psychological proclivities supporting truthfulness and prevarication but are too numerous to discuss here. For the interested reader I highly recommend Daniel Khaneman's seminal book, *Thinking Fast and Slow*.

My last topic for this chapter has to do with the overall relationship between psychology and Personnel Security-- which is largely complementary.

In the culture at large there is a tendency to default to the psychologist to explain phenomena we cannot understand. I have news for the reader—neither can we mental health professionals understand half of what is going on in the culture. The science is simply not mature enough to be as informative as we all would like and there is no disgrace in that. It is critical that we in the mental health field recognize this and we should be more forthcoming in discussing it. The DSM V is over 700 pages of diseases and disorders and no psychologist could possibly master all of these. Moreover, as science proceeds we make new discoveries-- which sometimes clarify issues and at other times muddle things. Again this is natural to the process of scientific advancement.

To offer a couple of pertinent examples, in 1971 homosexuality was designated as a disorder and in 1972 this designation was removed and same sex attraction became defined as an alternative lifestyle. In the 50s and 60s medical science treated ulcers as a stress and diet induced disorder with surgery as the primary treatment method; in the 70s we discovered ulcers were either a bacteriological infection or brought on by long-term use of non-steroidal anti-inflammatory drugs.[54] This is the way science works and the fact that change and new discovery is inevitable does not diminish the credibility of the field itself. Imagine if medical science had not changed from 1970 to today. Would that be an indicator of credibility? Of course not, it would be just the opposite. This recognition must be accompanied, however, by a sense of humility in the field and a willingness to say, "We don't know."

Indeed a 2015 paper, a sort of study of the studies, found that only 40% of studies in the field of psychology were replicable.[55] The capacity to replicate a study is fundamental to the credibility of what we do and we in the mental health field must do better.

One final example of appropriate scientific humility is offered by Martin Seligman, former president of the American Psychological Association (APA.) In arguing for more aggressive gun control laws he states.

"I have found that drugs and therapy offer disappointingly little additional help for the mentally ill than they did 25 years ago — despite billions of dollars in funding. **And there is zero promise that any developments I am aware of will help curb the violence that mentally ill persons commit**. (Emphasis is my own) Crazy people and evil people can commit mass murder, and they always do it with guns. Our society's only real leverage, at least in the near term, lies in reducing access to guns."[56]

The above observation is important to the field of Personnel Security Screening because we must not only screen for spies, misfits and mass leakers but we are increasingly called upon to protect against mass shooters.

---

54 Chow, S, Ph.D. *Peptic Ulcer History,* News, Medical Life Sciences, 23 Aug 2018, Retrieved, 18 Sept 2019, https://www.news-medical.net/health/Peptic-Ulcer-History.aspx

55 Huston, M, *Notes from a Revolution,* Psychology Today, May/June 2019, P 80.

56 Seligman, M, *The Solution to Violence is Gun Control not Mental Health Reforms,* Center on Media Crime and Justice, 4 January, 2013, Retrieved, 18 Sept, 2019, https://thecrimereport.org/2013/01/04/2013-01-op-ed-solution-to-violence-is-gun-control-not-mental/

This entails the proverbial needle in a haystack conundrum. In a nation of nearly 320 million it is near impossible to identify the one tenth of one percent who may become mass shooters. We must, at a minimum, try.

One of the reasons I am spending so much time on the notion of imperfection and limits in the fields of psychiatry and psychology is that PS professionals tend to defer too much to mental health professionals. We ask them to identify potential mass shooters but to do so without any false positives i.e. falsely identifying someone as problematic when he is not. We are frequently asked to diagnose someone who does not have a disorder; they merely lack self-discipline and/or are just a pain in the ass. We are occasionally asked to logically explain behavior that is utterly illogical.

The PS professional should rely on the mental health professional for input. Sometimes, but only sometimes, that input will be a diagnosis. In any event, the PS officer must make the decision and not hand off the actual decision to the psychologist. This is particularly true of private therapists interviewed as a part of a background investigation who have no idea of national security issues but are often quick to try to impose their judgment. These mental health professionals differ from psychologists and psychiatrists who actually work in the national security field and face PS and counterintelligence cases on a regular basis. Based on real world experience, the latter tend to be more adept at handling PS issues.

This should surprise no one; physicians who specialize in cardiology and deal in heart disease everyday have more expertise in their specialty than an internist who practices general medicine. Similarly, psychologists who specialize in substance abuse gain more expertise in their field than a therapist who specializes in depressive disorders. Likewise national security psychologists become more familiar with issues touching on national security and consequently their comments tend to have more relevance and impact in the PS field.

In most cases the PS professional will not get a clean, neat and fully explanatory diagnosis. The real world consists of largely shades of gray and indeed most mental health treatment specialists treat not disorders but life problems. For example, there is no "Divorce Adjustment Disorder" but I can assure you that treatment specialists spend a great deal of time helping clients through divorces. Often the therapist will diagnose depression—which may well be the case.

I want to emphasize what I am about to write is NOT a matter of science; there are no studies to support my thesis. It is more a perception that will not often be seen in print but it is nonetheless important for the PS professional to understand.

In the late 80s Congress passed legislation to insure mental health issues were covered by insurance companies as physical health was/is. It took quite some time for full implementation of that goal and with good reason. As with coverage for physical ailments, the question of what should be covered and what should not be covered encompassed a vast territory and had to be worked out over many years.

Eventually, insurance companies decided to cover largely diagnosed disorders. Having trouble relating to people because of shyness now became a disorder, Social Anxiety Disorder as did sadness which now often became diagnosed as Depression. Similarly, conceit was redefined as Narcissism, a bad temper as Impulse Control disorder and, of course, addiction was redefined as Substance Abuse disorder.

Let me hasten to add that these redefinitions were quite often accurate and appropriate; many individuals were truly disordered and needed mental health assistance to get better. Various treatment modalities were generated by this move to define and diagnose and much in the way of scientific advancement also occurred. However, what started as healthy advancement designed to help mental health clients seemed to deteriorate into a rush to find a diagnosis so the insurance company could be billed. Many companies will not cover mental health "treatment" for job-related sadness but will cover dysthymia (mild depression) as long as the therapist defines the problem as dysthymia and not deep seated job-related unhappiness. This phenomenon is one reason that the number of pages in the DSM III increased by over a third from 1990 to 2019.

Let me also add that this occurrence was NOT the result of some conscious plot on the part of the mental health industry. No, this occurred because most in the mental health field are trained to view problematic behavior in a clinical light and define it as a disorder. Hence their instinct is to do just that. (This trend may have contributed to the "epidemic" of Depression and Narcissism)

This is important to the PS professional because she may seek a diagnosis when in fact the behavior may be overstated or over-interpreted. Disqualification resting on a diagnosis of a disorder has a lot more credibility than a description of bad behavior by the PS professional herself. Hence institutional pressure exists to use diagnosis by a mental health professional as a tool of adjudication rather than the PS officer evaluating on bad behavior alone. In short, as I tell my students, a disqualification based on a diagnosis will withstand scrutiny better than one without a diagnosis.

Conversely, there certainly are delicate situations which directly rely on the psychologist's area of expertise. Paraphilias (sexual disorders) and psychosis are but two examples of issues that require the expertise of the psychologist for proper evaluation.

The PS officer should rely on mental health specialists as one tool in an array of methods available to her. We also rely on intelligence and counterintelligence specialists, financial analysts and other security officers as sources of expertise to assist with investigations and adjudications. The PS officer needs to be careful not to become TOO dependent on the mental health field and essentially hand off adjudicative responsibilities.

CHAPTER SIX

PERSONNEL SECURITY AND CATASTROPHIC EVENTS

At this point I would like to remind the reader that the ultimate goal of Personnel Security vetting is to identify potential applicants who are trustworthy, loyal and reliable. In doing this vetting we rely heavily on probabilities, percentages and risk. We do this because there is no other way i.e. the study of human behavior is far from an exact science that lends itself to behavior prediction. Hence we must rely on probabilities.

Despite common perception, Personnel Security is NOT in the business of identifying spies or potential spies, mass leakers or potential mass leakers or mass shooters or potential mass shooters. Once again, if we could do this we would but there is no way of predicting such rare behaviors. What we do is try to make certain we hire people who are trustworthy, reliable and honest. If we do that, we reduce the probability that we will have spies, mass leakers or mass shooters in our population. Does this mean we disregard the possibility of employing these catastrophe-inclined individuals? Of course not but we recognize the pitfalls of screening for these people.

In the real world we need to be concerned about false positives. For example, one trait that is observed to be disproportionate in the population of mass shooters is domestic abuse. Specifically one expert suggests that 54% of all mass shooters have been involved in domestic violence either as a perpetrator or a victim. [57] Does it not follow that domestic abuse should be treated as a predictive factor in screening for future mass shooters? Well, no it does not.

PS personnel already screen for crime, and the commission of domestic violence is indeed a crime treated seriously by most police departments and courts—unlike years ago. It is a rather simple matter to include commission of domestic violence in any investigation and subsequent adjudication. Of course, the offense must be evaluated in context and with a healthy sense of proportion. Not all domestic violence is equal and, like any other crime, can often be mitigated somewhat by circumstances. One common domestic violence scenario lending itself to mitigation has both husband and wife inflicting minor injuries on each other in a scuffle, pressing cross complaints and then dropping the complaints the next day. I can attest to the frequency of such behaviors based on my own police experience.

To be clear on this point—we consider domestic violence a subset of the crime issue. When we learn of domestic violence we evaluate it in accordance with the Whole Person Concept i.e. gravity of the offense accompanied by mitigating factors, if any, and draw an adjudicative conclusion. Often we will deny based largely on this offense and ergo will reduce the statistical probability that we will hire a future mass shooter. The denial, however, is **not** based on the predictive capacity of the behavior per se; it is a conclusion as to overall reliability, trustworthiness and honesty and, in the national security arena, risk to national security. In other words the adjudicative statement is not: we think this subject may become a mass shooter someday, but rather

---

57 Spitzer, R, Interview on All Things Considered, Michel Martin, *The Relationship Between Domestic Violence And Mass Shootings*, 7 Oct 2017.

we think this person does not display a level of integrity that suggests reliability, trustworthiness and honesty sufficient to entrust him with a position of trust. (This will PROBABLY reduce the risk of hiring a mass shooter but to a minimal degree.)

In addition, we have the conundrum of a **victim** of domestic violence being more prone to committing domestic violence. Should we screen for victimhood and then eliminate some based on a statistical inference? We should not.

The false positive syndrome makes evaluation of these factors difficult. While it is certainly true that domestic violence is disproportionately present in the backgrounds of mass shooters, it is also true that the vast, vast majority of domestic violence perpetrators and victims are decidedly not at any significant risk for mass shooting. So—additional PS scrutiny for all of that population may result in ineffective use of resources but, worse, inappropriate examination of victims. Or does it?

The entire concept of PS screening is just that—reviewing large amounts of data for the presence of risk factors. Almost by definition, this review will result in no negative outcomes i.e. Any untoward behavior. For example, we scrutinize all PS subjects for crime knowing that the vast majority have never committed a crime. It is nonetheless, undeniably worthwhile to perform that scrutiny to confirm the absence of criminal activity—as best as that can be done. The confirmation of absence i.e. there is no crime in this subject's background is of enormous value. Indeed it is the bedrock of PS screening and of maximum value. It is the same with other risk factors in the PS arena.

The problem with screening for "predictive" factors is, as aforementioned, the substantial majority of subjects screened for domestic violence will never commit a mass shooting. Hence we need to also take into account the egregiousness of the behavior. If we note domestic violence of a more serious nature, i.e. it results in serious physical injury this is taken to be more suggestive of future risk than less serious domestic violence.

It is a truism that rare events like terrorist activities, mass leaking and espionage are enormously hard to predict. We do not like to accept that fact because in doing so we surrender a feeling of control. We **want** to believe that we can predict these events so that we can feel safe. In addition, in today's media saturated environment, the instant there is a catastrophic event the media launches a quest to blame someone/something never recognizing the enormous odds facing agencies in trying to identify potential wrongdoers before the incident.

The reason it is so difficult to predict catastrophes is their rarity of occurrence. Of course, in accordance with the availability heuristic, saturation media coverage gives us the impression that these events are not rare and are commonplace. They are not.

If we look at mass shooting incidences they are almost always committed by a single person—out of a population of 320,000,000. Mental health issues are present in large numbers of the population that do this but there is little that can be done about this **before** the event. This is for the same reason as previously stated i.e. the vast majority of mental health sufferers will never be violent and to identify those that might commit a catastrophic event is a daunting, low-probability event. We are much more likely to identify many innocent people who present no real threat. In the immediate wake of 911, there were a handful of individuals who were misidentified as terrorists and sometimes questioned at length or even wrongly imprisoned.

As a nation that strongly supports civil rights, we are adamantly opposed to locking people up for deranged behavior. The one exception to that rule is in the case of an individual representing a threat to himself or someone else. In that case the police may forcibly remove an individual from the street or his house and have him evaluated by hospital mental health professionals. There again, the judgment to be made is the same: Is this person a danger to himself or another? More often than not, the judgment is made that the client is NOT a threat to anyone.

It is also quite difficult to predict future violence. In 2019, there was a mass shooting at Thousand Oaks California. Months prior to the shooting, police were called to the shooter's home. They evaluated the individual and decided to defer to the mental health professional on the team to do a further evaluation. The mental health specialist judged this person as no threat to himself or anyone else. Seven months later he shot and killed 12 people. [58]

In the Parkland shooting Nikolas Cruz posted on YouTube, "I'm going to become a professional school shooter." This posting was reported to the FBI who concluded the identity of the poster could not be confirmed. [59] The media made much of this but the reality is that there are literally millions of postings a day by millions of people many of whom use a false name. My point here is that even with some minimal degree of prior information it is nonetheless extremely difficult to identify these people in advance.

So let me repeat the basic mantra of personnel security: we screen people to identify only trustworthy, reliable and honest individuals. We cannot do any better than that and in doing that we reduce the probability that these individuals will partake in a catastrophic event. Since many catastrophically- inclined people have serious mental health issues, mental health screening is particularly important. So why, you ask do some well-screened, apparently stable people five years after

---

58 Levinson, E, Pagliery, J & de Puy Camp, M, Thousand Oaks shooter was a Marine veteran who often visited the site of the shooting, CNN Online, 8 Nov 2018, Retrieved 27 Sept 2019,

59 Loanes, E, *Police call Florida shooter's social media presence 'disturbing'* The Daily Dot, 16 Feb, 2018, Retrieved 30 Sept 2019, https://www.dailydot.com/layer8/florida-shooters-disturbing-social-media-presence/

screening get into all kinds of trouble? The answer is-- life happens.

Let's examine the case of Lisa Nowick, a female astronaut. Although this case is not a catastrophic event as defined herein, it nonetheless illustrates the difficulty in the vetting process. She attended the naval academy, graduated and did her time in the Navy. She performed very well, married, had children and rose to the level of astronaut—an elite position. All was well and she seemed to have all the accoutrements of trustworthiness, integrity, reliability and stability. In her early 40s she seemed to be headed for great things and, I suspect, if you asked her in advance if she would ever engage in an affair risking her marriage and career, she would have vehemently denied it. [60]

And then she had an affair with another male astronaut. The affair ended with the male having another affair with another female astronaut— which Ms. Nowick discovered. She was in Houston Texas when she decided to act on this recently acquired knowledge. She purchased a blackjack, mace, and an eight inch folding knife and then drove from Houston to Orlando Florida to confront her romantic rival. Upon confronting her, the rival fled, called police to the scene and Ms. Nowick was arrested. [61] Needless to say she lost both her marriage and her career.

The reader may be asking-- what issues did the psychological screening of Nowick miss and the answer is: none. Despite the fact that her lawyers conveniently claimed (after the fact) that she had Obsessive Compulsive Disorder and short term psychosis, she showed no signs of personality disorder prior to her affair. Because she had none.

Love/romance conflicts can be severe; I would estimate that murders of spurned/mistreated lovers happen on a daily basis. The emotions

---

60 Reed, T, 19 Sept 2007, AP, *Ex-Astronaut Wants Evidence Tossed Out*, Retrieved 30 Sept 2019, https://web.archive.org/web/20071026011659/http://apnews.myway.com/article/20070919/D8ROJMJ00.html
61 Ibid

are so strong that they can overpower even the mature, stable psycho-social restraint system—as was the case with Lisa Nowick. The restraint system simply is overcome by the passion of the event and the moment and otherwise stable people commit the most outrageous acts. One can see this everyday with our political leaders such as Anthony Weiner, Mark Sanford and Bill Clinton—to name but a few.

Despite the best efforts of the mental health industry to diagnose all irrational behaviors as pathology, not every senseless act, particularly a singular act, is the product of a disordered psyche. This is especially true in the area of love/lust which can short circuit rationality. What this says to the PS professional is that most catastrophic events are not predictable. One can do a thorough vetting job and later events can intervene to cause very untoward endings. I believe this is generally understood by most PS professionals but gravely misunderstood by the public.

CHAPTER SEVEN

RISK, PERCENTAGES, PROPORTIONALITY AND PROBABILITIES

It may not be an overstatement to claim that ALL major decisions are based on calculations of risk, percentages and probabilities. Buying a car, choosing a mate, deciding on a vacation, evaluating a job offer all have a plus/minus factor to be considered. When making these decisions we make guesses as to what will increase our well-being-- a kind of cost benefit calculation. Sometimes these decisions are no-brainers but more often we struggle with these decisions and outcomes are mixed. Who hasn't had the feeling at one time or another that, for example, I should have stayed with my previous employer.

In the national security theater and indeed in job considerations as well, no one has a constitutional right to a security clearance or a job. This is a bedrock criterion that is often misunderstood. Obviously, there are lots of qualifying laws and rules with the most salient being non-discrimination laws. Many of these laws apply equally to the PS field as they pertain to job approval/denial decisions. This requires some amplification.

When applying for a job at CIA, a security clearance is required; no one can be an employee of CIA without a clearance. Accordingly the PS unit has what amounts to a de facto veto in hiring. An individual make be a graduate of Harvard Law School and a superb attorney but she is not getting hired if she cannot pass the security vetting. This is also the case at other national security agencies.

Conversely, if one applies for a job at a large company, let's say company A, and is denied a security clearance for access to classified projects, the company may well have another position in the non-national security arena. In these cases denial of a security clearance may well **not** be a denial of employment. (To be perfectly honest, however, Company A may take substantial notice of the clearance denial and deny the job anyway.)

My point is there is often confusion between legal constructs regarding employment and criminal law protections. We need, and have, very high thresholds of evidence, due process and assumption of innocence in criminal matters. This is for good reason as a defendant's freedom and sometimes his life, in capital cases, is on the line. One of the core assumptions of our criminal justice system is: it is better to free nine guilty defendants than convict one innocent person. These principles are essential and, I dare say, supported by the vast majority of Americans.

Principles of employment are not as strident because what is at stake is a job—not a life. That is not to say that our laws ought to ignore the notion of hiring fairness; they shouldn't, but the levels of protection are, by design, not as strenuous as criminal protections. This is as it should be.

HR hiring decisions are among the most subjective and often equate to an individual merely liking the job applicant. Typically, absent possible violations of specific labor law, there is no appeals process. It is a system that invites cronyism and network hiring (old boy?) rather than true merit based hiring.

Firing decisions can be just as arbitrary with few safeguards in the non-union sector. Workers can be fired for highly subjective company violations or simply because the boss develops a dislike for a particular worker. Corporations that are sold frequently replace large numbers of workers with no explanation required and no consideration of impacts on the families of those terminated. (State labor laws vary but the above is a reasonable description of private, current hiring and firing processes in many states.)

PS decisions tend to be more heavily regulated than HR decisions and are based, to some extent, on probabilities, proportionality and percentages. An appeals process is built in, in which the subject has the right to appear himself, with or without an attorney. PS decisions are handicapped, however, by the aforementioned concern with invasiveness.

The PS community is in an ongoing, never-ending wrestling match with the conflict between invasiveness versus comprehensiveness. To delve too far into a person's background invites non-cooperation sometimes devolving into resistance. This is where a sense of proportion must reign supreme.

For example, the question on the SF 86 (questionnaire used for security clearance consideration) has recently changed the question on mental health counseling. The current question asks whether the person has:

Had a court or administrative agency declare them mentally incompetent

Been ordered by a court or administrative health agency to meet with a mental health professional

Been hospitalized due to a mental health condition

A mental or another type of health condition that has a significant adverse effect on judgment, reliability or trustworthiness

Had a health care professional issue a diagnosis of psychotic disorder, schizophrenia, schizoaffective disorder, delusional disorder, bipolar mood disorder, borderline personality disorder or antisocial personality disorder. [62]

This reconstruction of the mental health question is clearly an effort to be less invasive, more deferential, more fact-based and supportive to those seeking mental health counseling. All good, correct?

To illustrate the notion of proportionality in PS--perhaps the type of case that requires the most appropriate sense of proportion may be the person with Post Traumatic Stress Disorder (PTSD). Here we have the perfect example of the "sympathetic subject" i.e. someone almost everyone sympathizes with. Often this person has contracted the disorder in a combat zone defending his country, adding impetus to the sympathy factor. Who wants to say no to a job or a clearance for this person? Indeed there is room for sympathy in the adjudicative equation but it should not be singularly determinative.

PTSD, like most diseases and disorders, comes in degrees of severity. PTSD sufferers sometimes get a pension from the Veterans Administration (VA.) Those pensions vary from 10% to 100% depending on the severity of the affliction. [63] Contrary to many media representations, the vast majority of those with some degree of PTSD is observably functional and poses no threat to anyone or anything.

---

62 Psychological Health Question Has Changed in SF-86 Questionnaire, No author, https://www.keepyourclearance.com/news/sf-86-psychological-health-question-has-changed/

63 Veterans Law Group, Retrieved 5 Oct 2019, https://search.yahoo.com/search?p=veteranslaw.com&fr=uh-mail-web&fr2=p%3AmI%2Cm%3Asb.

The adjudicative default position should be to approve—obviously after consideration of all facts of the case.

We should nonetheless not bypass the adjudication process because we feel for this subject. Some subjects in the IC receive a clearance and carry a weapon. CIA, DOD and others have their own armed police force. We cannot give a weapon and access to sensitive facilities and people to anyone because we feel sorry for them. No, cold reason combined with reasonable empathy must prevail.

This is easier said than done. I myself have been involved in adjudicating cases similar to this and it is exceedingly difficult to remain objective; the urge to approve based on empathy is strong indeed. In fact empathy SHOULD be a part of the adjudicative equation; I would not want to live in a PS world where it was not. The PS professional must never de-humanize the task; she should always remember that we are dealing with real people, real lives and the impact we have can often be either exhilarating or emotionally debilitating.

The core point must remain however—PS decisions must result from a mixture of empathy and reason. One should not dominate the other, especially in the case of the sympathetic subject. This brings us to the issue of risk-- which is closely associated with proportionality.

Immediately after 911, many citizens understandably chose to drive rather than fly. Indeed, the President halted all commercial air traffic until the government could develop some sense of what happened and introduce basic security countermeasures. Unsurprisingly, air travel dropped precipitously and automobile traffic rose significantly.

Virtually all studies show that air travel in general, is much safer than car travel. According to three different studies, the increase in auto travel and decrease in air travel after 911 resulted in anywhere from 317 to

1,018 more deaths in the three months following 911.[64] Obviously, at that time, almost no one was dispassionately reasoning; reason was temporarily displaced by plain old fear and air travel dropped drastically while deaths from car travel increased.

Israel is closely associated with terrorist activities. Between December 2001 and September 2004 there were 23 suicide bombings producing 236 fatalities. Israeli citizens use buses about 1.3 million times a day. The risk of injury or death due to a suicide bombing was infinitesimal yet the Israelis avoided buses like the plague in that period.[65]

These events perfectly describe the risk/benefit calculation—or more accurately how the risk/benefit calculation can be tainted by the emotional non-thinking produced by the availability heuristic. As a result of 911, Americans placed themselves in a much higher risk pool (driving) while removing themselves from a lower risk population (flyers) So- a singular catastrophic event propelled Americans to unknowingly assume greater risk in their travels. In this case 911 may be described as the most substantial availability heuristic ever. For months thereafter the media saturated the airwaves with coverage almost all of it with focusing on the utter human tragedy of the event. I am not criticizing that coverage; it was highly appropriate and satisfied a dire need at the time.

It does illustrate, however, the difficulty in evaluating and acting upon risk calculations. I took a cruise about 6 months after 911 and encountered a smart, savvy fellow traveler. He advised me he booked his cruise two days after 911 and the price was about 70% less than what I paid for the same cruise.

The human psyche is NOT a robotic calculator applying hard logic to PS decisions. No, they are impacted by emotion-- as many other

---

64 Ropeik, D. (2010) How Risky is it, Really? McGraw Hill, NY, P 66
65 Kahneman, P 322

decisions are. The hope is to minimize the emotional input (most frequently associated with the availability heuristic) and come to a logical, empathy risk based and proportional outcome.

Khaneman discusses this issue at length stating algorithms tend to be better assessors of behavior than individuals. This is due to the Optimism Bias i.e. we think we are better at such judgments than we really are. PS professionals might assign too much validity to their own instincts and too little to countermanding variables. [66]

Am I suggesting that algorithms should be used to adjudicate cases? No, I am not suggesting this exclusively but more algorithm-like analysis might be more productive. For example, adjudicative data might be placed into an algorithm and used as an aid to the adjudicator's final decision. This might limit the impact of Optimism Bias and reduce subjectivity overall. It could serve as a kind of second opinion demanding consideration of all factors of the case--weighted appropriately.

Risk assessment can be very effective if used in a rational way. When we have singular catastrophic events like a plane crash, reason takes a very distant second to emotion. The worst plane crash in history occurred in 1977 in Tenerife, Canary Islands when two jumbo jets collided on the runway killing 583 people. Compare this to the death toll in the U.S. from heart disease which totals about 1,800 **a day.** The gradual, non-spectacular deaths evoke little emotion and hence risk analysis for heart disease is more reasoned and less tainted by emotion. [67] In the immediate aftermath of the Tenerife crash calm risk assessment was all but impossible.

To provide a hypothetical example in the PS world, if an agency has a rash of suicides, the mental health teams may come to evaluate suicidal statements (with no corresponding action) more substantively than

---

66 Ibid, P 225
67 Roepik, P 105

they might otherwise. In the wake of a big spy case adjudicators may tend to lean toward the denial side of the equation if they observe anything similar to the spy case. Thresholds of tolerance may change overnight based on little more than one spectacular event which may or may not provide PS related information. You did not want to have a reinvestigation polygraph scheduled at CIA immediately after the Aldridge Ames case broke. Such events awaken and reinforce the Precautionary Principle which tilts us toward safety and intolerance of behavior we might otherwise accept.

Lastly, I want to discuss context of behavior, without which behavior cannot be properly evaluated. It is meaningless to singularly state that a subject has been arrested for a felony and therefore he should be disapproved.

In the aforementioned Aaron Alexis case, he was arrested for Criminal Mischief in Seattle, Washington. Alexis engaged some construction workers in a discussion about their parked car adjacent to his residence. The discussion devolved into an argument and Alexis shot out the tires of the car. He was subsequently arrested and referred to the Seattle Municipal court; the charge was dismissed for lack of evidence.[68] This arrest was known to the DOD adjudicative unit at the time of consideration for a clearance and the initial Secret clearance was granted. A clear case of gross negligence—right? Not so quickly.

Alexis was interviewed about this incident but stated he "deflated" the tires of the construction workers—a statement that is literally true.[69] The interviewer accepted Alexis' version unaware of the use of the gun for the deflation and went on to approve the clearance. Well, this certainly proves negligence in not following up—does it not? No—it does not.

---

68 Internal review of the Washington Navy Yard Shooting, A Report to the Secretary of Defense, 20 Nov, 2013, Retrieved, 14 Oct 2019, P 19. https://archive.defense.gov/pubs/Navy-Investigation-into-the-WNY-Shooting_final-report.pdf
69 Ibid, P 12

At the time, Seattle PD, as well as numerous other police departments around the country, did not share law enforcement data with non-law enforcement agencies. This was and is commonplace based on the confidentiality of such data. I would also add the old aphorism, *knowledge is power*, certainly adds fuel to this fire i.e. Agencies like to have exclusive knowledge and sharing it makes it not exclusive. So, the investigator contacted Seattle PD and was told, politely and diplomatically, to get lost. Had the context of the act been known it may well have been the case that Alexis would have been denied a clearance. This was, after all, a felony with a gun. (Seattle PD, largely as a result of this case, has changed its policy and now shares arrest data with federal government clearance investigators.) As this case amply illustrates, one cannot evaluate behavior in context if one does not have all the necessary data.

To summarize, all PS decisions, like most decisions, are really statements of risk i.e. John is a good risk to properly handle a sensitive position. While the requested "answer" is indeed bipolar, hire or not, the real answer speaks to percentages and probability. It is also sometimes the case that a PS action may be executed and judged well but three years later the subject has life changing events which convert him from low risk to high risk. As an example, many divorces are highly taxing and can change an individual and place so much stress on him as to produce poor decisions. This is why it is critical to maintain a robust reinvestigation program equipped with Continuous Evaluation.

Hopefully, PS decisions will be right considerably more often than they are wrong. It is, however, the nature of the beast that some calls will be wrong. This can unconsciously push decision makers in the direction of "safe" determinations. Those so called safe outcomes are denials because-- if you grant no one a job or a clearance you cannot be proven wrong. More commonly, this is not a clear, zero/sum equation, rather the risk calculation is tilted in the direction of denials. The community must strenuously guard against this mode of thinking.

CHAPTER EIGHT

SUBSTANCE USE AND ABUSE

At this point I will begin to discuss the more commonplace behaviors encountered in the PS world. Not all of the previously listed Adjudicative Guidelines occur with the same frequency and impact. I will start with the issue of substance use/abuse.

The term *addiction* is the common term used in the culture to refer to someone who is experiencing difficulty in handling substances. The clinical term is dependence, which is defined as follows:

A maladaptive pattern of substance use leading to clinically significant impairment or distress, as manifested by three or more of the following in a 12 month period: 1) tolerance, 2) withdrawal, 3) continued use despite cognizance of the problem, 4) persistent, unsuccessful attempts to cut down, 5) significant time spent pursuing the substance, 6) important social, occupational or recreational activities are eliminated or reduced, 7) the substance is often taken in larger amounts and over a longer period than was intended. [70]

Abuse is a lower level of substance use difficulty which is defined as:

---

[70] DSM IV TR, American Psychiatric Association, Arlington VA, 2005, P 197

A maladaptive pattern of substance use leading to clinically significant impairment or distress, as manifested by one or more of the following in a 12 month period: 1) recurrent use resulting in failure to fulfill role obligations (work, school) 2) use generating physical hazard (driving, machinery) 3) legal problems, 4) social or interpersonal problems (marriage, friends) [71]

These definitions are the definitive descriptions of abuse and dependence as taken from the DSM used by psychiatrists and psychologists. Individual clinicians often write books and/or papers offering their own definitions which sometimes are embraced by the media culture. These definitions often focus on compulsive craving—which is certainly present. It is important to note, however, that these cravings do NOT constitute grounds for claiming loss of control due to ANY disorder. The culture at large seems to imply, or state outright, that an individual may not be ABLE to control his/her behavior, this is a critical point. The DSM V states, *Even when diminished control over one's behavior is a feature of the disorder, having the diagnosis in itself does not demonstrate that a particular individual is (or was) unable to control his or her behavior at a particular time.* [72]

This is very important to any PS professional because we very often hear the lament that one cannot control one's behavior and hence they are not accountable. This is nonsense. We are all responsible for our actions and the presence of a disorder does not reduce the degree of responsibility. Sometimes this plea is made directly but more often the society simply tilts in the direction of non-responsibility and tolerates more than it should.

Once again the drug dependent individual may be (or may not be) a sympathetic figure but in all cases there is only one individual who can enter treatment and that is the drug user himself. Likewise, there is

---

71 Ibid, P 199
72 Ibid, P xxxiii

only one person who can determine success in treatment and that is the user himself.

Moreover, based on my own experience, the IC encounters few drug dependent individuals. By a large majority, the users we deal with are recreational drug users who are not dependent. This may be due to self-screening i.e. potential employees know that the IC, and the government in general, aggressively screen for substance use/abuse and hence do not apply. In addition, many substance abusers have other mental health issues, some of which may result in observable undesirable behaviors which further discourage them from making application.

So-- the issue most commonly grappled with by the IC is not addiction/dependence but recreational use. How do we manage that?

Collecting information on someone's drug use is difficult largely because investigative sources are reluctant to provide such information. Some may not be aware of use but others may be cognizant and do not want to "report" on friends/acquaintances. This brings us to a major obstacle in PS processing in general-- but particularly in the area of substance use/abuse.

We have a deep, inbred cultural instinct against this type of information provision. Since we were children it has been pounded into our psyche to not "rat." Sammy the Bull Gravano testified against Mafia chief John Gotti, a person who essentially engaged in multiple murders for power and money. The day after his testimony the NY Daily News led with the headline, *I am a RAT*.[73]

Whitey Bulger, a Boston Irish gangster readily admitted to murder, large scale drug sales, extortion and many other crimes but steadfastly

---

[73] NY Dailey News Headline *I am a Rat*, page 1, 6 March, 1992, Retrieved 20 Oct 2019, https://www.gettyimages.com/detail/news-photo/daily-news-front-page-march-6-sammy-bull-im-a-rat-gravano-news-photo/97298862

denied he was an FBI informant—which he was.[74] He was grossly embarrassed by the charge of informing but less embarrassed by allegations torturing and killing people. That is how firmly embedded this reticence to report is.

Let me add some context to this discussion. I am not advocating reporting on a colleague when she leaves work an hour early on Friday or calls in sick when she is not ill. A reasonable sense of proportion makes this clear but reporting on someone who is hoarding classified information should be treated quite differently. Conversely, as reported in a previous chapter, John Walker's wife contacted the FBI about his wrongdoing which eventually led to his arrest and conviction for espionage. Unlike in the Walker case, this common reticence to advise security officials of substantial wrongdoing makes the job of the PS professional much more difficult.

Returning to my main theme, PS evaluates recreational drug use for the very same reasons it evaluates other behaviors—to determine if this activity is reflective of an absence of honesty, integrity and trustworthiness. Usually, but not always (and depending on the overall context) use of small amounts of illegal drugs well in a person's past is not considered an indicator of such deficiencies. In general the evaluative criteria used to make judgments include: type of substance, recency of use, frequency of use, intensity of use, reason for discontinuance (if applicable) treatment sought or completed and time length since treatment completion (if applicable). These evaluators apply to alcohol abuse as well. I must add that without the use of a polygraph, it almost impossible to reliably ascertain and confirm these criteria. In the absence of polygraph derived data PS officers must evaluate what they have while remaining cognizant that they may well NOT have the full picture. Self-reported substance abuse data is notoriously underreported for the most obvious reason. Nonetheless, adjudicators

---

74 Raddan-Keith, P, *Assets and Liabilities*, The New Yorker, 21 Sept 2005, Retrieved 20 Oct, 2019, https://www.newyorker.com/magazine/2015/09/21/assets-and-liabilities

must adjudicate on what they have, not what they wish they had.

Since several states have legalized or decriminalized marijuana, use of marijuana by applicants has become more controversial. In a 2014 executive document signed by then DNI James Clapper, he stated that marijuana use still violates Federal law and hence the legality in certain states is immaterial for purposes of clearance approval or denial. [75] All marijuana use must be reported and evaluated.

It is important to note that legality or illegality of use is NOT dispositive. We currently evaluate alcohol use, financial irresponsibility, mental health issues etc. none of which are illegal. Illegality should be one factor considered among many when adjudicating a case. The illegality may speak to one's unwillingness to adhere to laws and hence a capacity for restraint. The adjudicator may reasonably infer that the subject's unwillingness to obey certain laws could suggest an overall predisposition toward nonconformance to workplace laws and regulations. Moreover, in the case of drugs but not alcohol, the sole purpose of using a drug is to alter the mind i.e. to get high. One can have one glass of wine with dinner with no intent to get high but there is no point in smoking a joint without getting high. Lastly, use of drugs illegally may speak to willingness to assume risk—perhaps unreasonable risk on the part of the subject. This is yet another potential factor in the adjudicative equation.

When discussing marijuana today it is impossible to not address medical marijuana. Medical marijuana has been legal in many states for years and its ostensible use is commonplace. Let me start this discussion by addressing the elephant in the room i.e. is the medical marijuana use under examination really for medical purposes or is it a cover for recreational use? This is a core question that must be

---

75 Clapper, J, *Adherence to Federal Laws Prohibiting Marijuana Use*, 25 Oct 2014.
 Retrieved 21 Oct 2019, https://www.employmentlawobserver.com/assets/htmldocuments/Blogs/EmploymentLawObserver/dni-memo-20fed-laws-prohibiting-marijuana-use.pdf

addressed by PS personnel.

There are two elements of marijuana we are concerned with: THC and CBD. THC is the psychoactive ingredient that gets one high. To date there has been no credible research to support any medical use of this substance. To be sure, one can find studies here or there claiming medicinal properties but these claims are, at best, untested. Conversely CBD is the ingredient found in marijuana that does have medicinal use but it does not get one high.

CBD derived from the marijuana plant has shown some promise in treating nausea resulting from chemotherapy. In some cases standard anti-nausea pharmaceuticals may not work for some unfortunate patients battling cancer and marijuana has shown some promise. Indeed there is currently a bill in the house to prohibit the Secretary of Veterans Affairs from denying a veteran benefits resulting from the veteran participating in a State-approved marijuana program. [76] While use for anti-nausea in chemotherapy has not yet been approved by the FDA, its use in such cases certainly falls under the umbrella of medical use and hence comes with a greater tolerance from a clearance/hiring perspective.

Conversely, the reader may be shocked, shocked to hear that many users of medical marijuana are really recreational users!! The PS officer must make a determination as to whether the use is truly medical or otherwise. As always, there is no magic formula to do this so we are stuck with a series of questions we use to help in making a determination as to credibility.

What is the medical condition? The FDA approved two cannabinoid based medicines -- dronabinol and nabilone to treat nausea and vomiting from chemotherapy. The cannabidiol drug Epidiolex was

---

[76] *Veterans Cannabis Use for Safe Healing Act* Cosponsor: 10/15/2019: Rep. Neguse, Joe [D-CO-2]

approved in 2018 for treating seizures associated with two rare and severe forms of epilepsy, Lennox-Gastaut syndrome and Dravet syndrome.[77]

These are the only truly legitimate medical uses of marijuana. Having said this, the PS professional's first question of a subject claiming medical use should be to confirm one of the medically approved usages. Use for anxiety, glaucoma, muscle relaxants, etc. Are not approved and should therefore be immediately suspect.

The next question is: *do you have a prescription and where did you get it?* Absent a prescription there is a very strong presumption of recreational, not medical usage. Of course many individuals may CLAIM that their usage helps with muscular tightness and it might. This may be due to either the placebo effect or a level of overall relaxation which includes muscle tissue. Nonetheless the claim is not credible. As a parallel, there are many old jokes about alcoholics using booze for "medicinal purposes only" and how credible are those claims?

Where did you get your prescription-- is important because there are many marijuana mills around the country who use doctors on site to "prescribe" standard marijuana. Those operations, while legal, reduce the validity of the claim because the intent of those mills is blatantly, obviously NOT to treat medically.

How did you ingest the marijuana? There are no legitimate medical uses wherein the substance is smoked. Generally marijuana is prescribed as drops or pills and to state one smoked it is to drastically reduce the credibility of the user.

What dosage was used? Most CBD oils employ about 10-20 milligrams of CBD while research in the field employs about 500 milligrams. This, in all probability, negates any positive effects of the

---

[77] Web MD, *Is medical marijuana FDA approved?* 15 Dec 2018, retrieved 22 Oct 2019, https://www.webmd.com/a-to-z-guides/qa/is-medical-marijuana-fda-approved

CBD product, short of the Placebo Effect. CBD oils drawn from both hemp and marijuana are legal although the ingredients used by various companies may vary widely—to include some low levels of THC which transposes the product from legal to illegal.

Why did you stop using marijuana? This is asked to evaluate the reasonableness of the response. Answers like--I graduated from HS, I finished college, I got into physical fitness tend to add credibility. Answers like I didn't like it (after using for years) are generally not credible. Let us now turn to today's number one crisis, the opioid epidemic which indeed makes concern with marijuana use seem insignificant.

The word, epidemic, is grossly overused but in this case it is apt. Opioid deaths peaked at 70,237 in 2017. [78] We have had a steady increase from 1999 to 2017 after which a small decrease occurred. In the 1990s, the cultural and medical emphasis on pain and pain relief resulted in overproduction and over-prescription of opioids. Powerful pharmaceuticals such as fentanyl, restricted primarily to the surgical suite and treatment for battlefield and battlefield-like injuries, began appearing in the black market.

Although a source of strong controversy today, the drugs were initially thought to be relatively non-addictive and were approved for restricted use by the FDA. [79] This proved to be inaccurate and the epidemic ensued.

For the PS professional there are a few questions that should be used to evaluate opioid use:

---

78 Center for Disease Control and Prevention (CDC) National Center for Health Statistics, 1999-2017, Retrieved 24 Oct 2019, https://en.wikipedia.org/wiki/Opioid_epidemic_in_the_United_States

79 Food and Drug Administration home page, Timeline of Selected FDA Activities and Significant Events Addressing Opioid Misuse and Abuse, 25 Sept 2019, Retrieved 24 Oct 2019, https://www.fda.gov/drugs/information-drug-class/timeline-selected-fda-activities-and-significant-events-addressing-opioid-misuse-and-abuse

Did you first use opioids with a prescription? If so, was the prescription supplied as a result of a prior medical procedure? If so, please describe the procedure.

Was the prescription provided by your private physician, a specialist or a previously unused doctor?

How old were you when you first used the drug?

Did you experience euphoria from use of the drug?

*Did you take the medication **as prescribed** or in some other way i.e. ground and snorted, liquefied and injected and/or in greater quantity than prescribed?*

Did you ever provide your prescription drugs to anyone else?

Did you ever obtain the drug from a source other than a prescription?

When is the last time you used an opioid?

How frequently did you use the drug?

Did you become addicted?

Did you receive treatment for addiction? If so, where? Describe the program. If not, how did you stop using opioids?

Is there anything else the record might show and you should tell me about your experience with opioids?

Obviously, as the above questions suggest, the PS professional must ascertain whether the opioid use was executed as medically ordered or otherwise. Contrary to media accounts, addiction from use as medically prescribed is not the norm. [80] Hence the above questions are critical in evaluating opioid use in the PS arena.

Once the context of the use is established (assuming it can be established) an adjudicative recommendation can be made. Once again, the bottom line question is: does this behavior suggest any deficiency and/or risk relative to the reliability, trustworthiness and integrity of the person being considered. It is not a moral judgment.

Let us now turn to a brief discussion of alcohol use and abuse.

As aforementioned there are two primary differences between drug use and alcohol use. Alcohol is legal and thus has lesser legal risk associated with it and drug's sole purpose is to get high. One can have a glass of wine with dinner and it has no effect on one's mood, driving ability, thinking capacity or anything else. One can have one beer at lunch and go back to worked unaffected; not so with marijuana, cocaine, crack, methamphetamine etc.

Conversely, very few drugs, with the exception of methamphetamine, elevate the risk of physical aggression. Alcohol is closely associated with violent behavior; domestic abuse survivors report that two thirds of their perpetrators were under the influence of alcohol. [81] Once again context and perspective is important.

Alcohol does not **cause** violent behavior; it increases the risk that violence will eventuate. This is one of the primary reasons we screen for alcohol use in the PS process. Of course, the vast majority of alcohol users do not become violent and handle drinking quite well. Frequent intoxication also elevates the risk of other untoward outcomes like

---

80 Noble, M, Treadwell, J. R, Tregear, S. J, Coates, V. H, Wiffen, P. J., Akafomo, C, Schoelles, K. M. (2010). Noble, Meredith (ed.). "Long-term opioid management for chronic noncancer pain". Cochrane Database of Systematic Reviews (1): CD006605.

81 T, Buddy, The Very Well Mind, *The Combination of Domestic Abuse and Alcohol*, 18 Sept 2019, Retrieved 25 Oct 2019, https://www.verywellmind.com/domestic-abuse-and-alcohol-62643

interpersonal conflict, marital difficulties and legal problems—to name a few. It can impede good judgment-- as the reader has no doubt observed on more than one occasion. Indeed, 60% of males and 30% 0f females have had one or more adverse life event due to alcohol. There are 15 diagnosable alcohol related disorders listed in the DSM V. [82] Sometimes (like illegal drug use) it results in disorders such as Alcohol Dependence (addiction) or Alcohol Abuse.

When the PS professional evaluates alcohol related behavior it is important to understand the extent and etiology of the activity. The usual types of inquiry should be made, frequency, recency, conduct change, if any, while under the influence, driving and/or other legal difficulties. Frequency and recency are paramount in this case; an individual who gets intoxicated once per year on New Year's Eve and does not drive nor engage in any other undesirable behavior is exhibiting relatively benign behavior revealing no diminution of trustworthiness, reliability or integrity. If the intoxication is more frequent the potential for adjudicative concern increases accordingly.

In addition, a question about drinking and violent behavior should **always** be asked. If the frequency is pronounced, further inquiry about possible alcoholism should ensue. It is important to point out that there is no amount threshold which is alerting. While excessive consumption is a concern, the definition of excessive is relative to the **effects** of the amount. Some large males may easily consume 5/6 beers at a sitting and not be affected while a smaller male may be intoxicated with the same amount consumed.

If an alcohol related disorder is suspected a clinician should be consulted to make the final determination. If a clinician is not available an adjudicative judgment may still be made based on behavior—not diagnosis.

---

[82] DSM IV, *Alcohol Related Disorders*, American Psychiatric Association, 2005, P 212

Treatment is, of course relevant to the adjudicative issue of substance use/abuse. I will repeat my prior statement that in my own experience in the IC we encountered few subjects battling addiction. Rather we faced largely recreational use and a large range of frequency and recency of recreational use. One DOD study relying on self-reporting found that only 1% of active duty personnel used illicit drugs in the past year.[83] This may be due to mandatory, intermittent urinalysis which likely serves as a strong deterrent. This is NOT to state that addiction in the society in general is not an issue—it certainly is. It is merely to note that addiction in the PS world is likely less prevalent.

Unfortunately, in the culture at large, discussions of treatment often deteriorate into bipolar arguments of treatment versus incarceration. This is unfortunate and I will not duplicate those discussions here but I will say that both options have their place.

I will also not attempt to quote voluminous statistics to "prove" that treatment works or it does not. There are a lot of data supporting both sides of the argument. What I will say is that treatment has its place as does incarceration. A two pronged approach is probably best but since the vast majority of substance use cases in the PS world do not involve cases of treatment. Consequently I will not spend a lot of time on treatment-related cases. Suffice to say, anyone who has undergone recent treatment tends to be placed in the category of higher risk. Conversely, if the treatment occurred 10 years ago and the subject is still abstinent, the case is placed in the lower risk bucket. Treatment can be miraculous for some people but PS professionals need to be aware of its limitations; while it is certainly mitigating, it is not a panacea. As previously stated, National Institute on Drug Analysis (NIDA) data suggests that 40 to 60% of those treated relapse. It is also true that the longer a person is abstinent the better the risk

---

[83] National Institute on Drug Abuse, No author, *Substance Abuse in the Military*, Oct 2019, Retrieved 27 Oct, 2019, https://www.drugabuse.gov/publications/drugfacts/substance-abuse-in-military

from a security perspective (This is true, in part, from reduced cravings.) [84]

From a PS perspective, when evaluating the much more common cases of recreational drug use, recency, frequency and type of substance are the paramount adjudicative considerations. We encounter a lot of recreational use while in high school or college and substance abuse is more male, and young. As individuals mature the recreational use of drugs and the overuse of alcohol tend to decline.

Ages 18-20 are the peak years for drug use followed but a steady decline in subsequent years. [85]

This is an important datum for PS personnel as the percentages and probabilities suggest greater risk at a younger age. In addition, substance abuse is more common in males than females giving yet another probability to be infused into the PS fabric. Overall, the use of illegal drugs and misuse of alcohol are issues to be considered within the concept of the whole person. As a general proposition, we tend to be quite tolerant of use/abuse by the young as long as there has been a reasonable period of abstention immediately prior to the clearance/hiring decision. Conversely, marijuana use by 50 year olds tends to frowned upon by PS professionals as age inappropriate behavior.

Sales of drugs should always be taken seriously but defined into two categories: sales for profit versus sales of small amounts to friends for purposes of recreational use. Frequency and amounts sold are priority considerations and, quite obviously sales for profit are near disqualifying in and of themselves while infrequent sales of very small amounts to friends is less concerning—depending on the facts of the case.

---

84 Very Well Mind, Early Abstinence From Drugs and Alcohol,
85 Bing Images, Age and Drug Use, Retrieved, 27 Oct, 2019, https://www.bing.com/images/search?q=age+and+drug+use&qpvt=age+and+drug+use&form=IGRE&first=1&cw=1129&ch=473

I would like to close this chapter with a brief discussion of the underlying conditions stimulating the epidemic of drugs-- particularly opioids. There is no shortage of explanations starting with poverty, income inequality, political oppression, family dissolution and the absence of self-discipline and restraint. To some extent, all of these may contribute but my focus here is on a creeping socioeconomic alienation.

Timothy Carne recently wrote a book, *Alienated America*, which focuses not on drug abuse per se but on the deterioration of the basic institutions that have substantially contributed to the amazing success of America. Marriage, the family, work, faith in government and religion are all in decline and those institutions have provided the bedrock of the social support system. He speaks of a sense of purposelessness born of an aimless social isolation and reliance on online, often anonymous, sources for support. He is worth quoting, *When you read the tales of opioid ravaged towns, you see that drugs often come in where people lack purpose.* [86]

While the conditions of social decline leading to drug abuse may not be in the direct purview of the PS officer, it is nonetheless useful to have some frame of reference in considering substance use/abuse cases. Carne provides just such a framework.

I provide special attention to substance use/abuse because it is one of the most frequent behaviors the PS officer encounters. The impact of drug and alcohol use varies from severe outcomes to completely benign and those outcomes need to be carefully evaluated.

---

86 Carne, T, (2019) *Alienated America*, Harper Collins, NY, P 116

CHAPTER NINE

FINANCES

Other than substance use/abuse, financial issues are the most common issues confronting PS professionals and they account for a very large share of denials and revocations. Since the U.S. culture at large has enormous credit and debt issues this should come as no surprise. Indeed, U.S. household debt increased from 43% to 62% of GDP from 1982 to 2000 and is commonly believed to have been a major contributing factor to the recession of 2007-2008. [87]

Many insurance companies use an individual's record of financial responsibility/irresponsibility to predict overall reliability and insurance risk. Specifically, Allstate Insurance examined the credit histories of 60,000 policyholders and found that those with substantial credit problems cost the company 40 per cent more in claims. [88] This implies that one's financial discipline may be suggestive of an overall responsibility. While many spies have committed espionage with money as their primary motivation, the PS professional nonetheless evaluates money management posture as yet another indicator of overall reliability, trustworthiness and integrity.

---

87 Wikipedia, https://en.wikipedia.org/wiki/Household_debt, Retrieved 30 Oct 2019.
88 Boundy, D. (1993). When money is the drug, The compulsion for credit cash and chronic debt. NY: Harper Collins.

The two primary money issues for PS professionals are debt and unexplained affluence. The two are different in that debt represents a vulnerability but unexplained affluence is more an alerting factor calling our attention to something that might be a result of illegal or untoward behavior. A subject may be a serious drug dealer, a spy or an embezzler and her affluence may be explained by such behavior. Hence unexplained affluence may be more an observable symptom rather than a risk factor. In either case robust PS screening is in order.

As the above datum suggests, Americans are awash in debt and the expansion of consumer debt has substantially contributed to our rate of economic growth. Since the 1950s the enormous increase of credit cards, mortgages and auto loans proved a boon to the American family. They promoted home ownership, mobility and easy access to evolving credit without which much of our prosperity would not have occurred. But, as the Great Recession illustrated, too much credit and credit improperly managed, can lead us down the path of destruction. I dare say managing money today is more difficult than in the prior generation—despite the fact that this generation has more credit (and therefore more spending power) than ever before.

The vulnerability presented by excessive debt is fairly obvious. An opposition intelligence service, a drug pusher, a loan shark all present different threats associated with debt. Spies such as Aldridge Ames, Robert Hanssen, Brian Regan and John Walker all committed espionage largely for money. Money can be a very powerful tool in espionage cases because it can ostensibly represent an **instant** solution. The enormous problem of debt can represent an extreme burden, psychological and otherwise, and can be relived in **one** payment made in **one** day. This instant solution compares to **years** of struggling with debt payment/repayment necessitating harsh material denial to oneself and family. This is one side of the issue.

Another side is money as a symbol of success. As previously stated,

Aldridge Ames stated outright he did it for the money because money provided evidence of success/non-failure. We Americans do not like to admit it but money does indeed represent success and the absence of money can denote failure.

This case was a historic pivotal point in the history of the IC and Personnel Security processing. Prior to the Ames case, security professionals focused almost exclusively on debt and rarely if ever on the notion of unexplained affluence. It simply did not occur to us to ask the question of why **this person doesn't** have debt normally associated with his financial situation. This deficit changed after the Ames case and agencies began to focus equally on both sides of the ledger.

The ideal program employs a financial disclosure form completed by an applicant or the subject of a periodic reinvestigation. The software can then automatically calculate income to debt ratio and net worth analysis. Once again, those two calculations should be consonant with an individual's financial stature. If an individual making $33,000 per year has a net worth of one million, an alert is activated and an investigation ensues. Most often, a reasonable explanation is found (inheritance for example) and no further action is required. This is the ideal approach to financial investigations.

In a conversation with the writer, Bob Hanssen was asked what might have deterred him and/or identified him as a spy. He quickly responded that a quality financial investigation policy would have deterred him. He also said that, as a converted Catholic, it was very important to him to educate his six children in Catholic schools—an enormously expensive proposition.[89] To be unable to send his children to Catholic schools represented true failure to Hanssen and drove him, in part, to espionage.

In our culture, money is the close cousin of power. Money is certainly

---

89 Thompson, T (2009) *Why Espionage Happens*, Seaboard Press, South Carolina, P 18

NOT synonymous with power but it usually provides a path to it. More importantly, however, money frequently provides status.

We obviously cannot walk around with our W-2 pasted to our forehead nor do we routinely advise people how much we make. That is simply not done and is considered tacky at best. So our spending patterns tend to shout out our degree of success. We buy flashy cars, houses with more space than we will ever need and take vacations that we cannot afford. Millionaires work very hard to become multi-millionaires and billionaires work equally hard to become multi-billionaires. Why?

Some of us reach a comfortable income and say—enough. Often, but not always, after reaching that comfort level a pause ensues only to be followed by a quest for more money because status needs predominate. Moreover, status is something we can NEVER talk about thereby making this issue even more difficult to handle.

The PS professional needs to understand how status seeking drives money accumulation and how that can be problematic. By any account Aldridge Ames had a comfortable income (GS 14) with a relatively high status job—case officer for CIA. Unfortunately, he fell in love with a higher status person and this drove his need for money and status. His second wife Rosario came from an influential Columbian family (her father was a government minister) and he had to measure up. No longer were $100.00 suits adequate; now he needed $500.00 suits and $200.00 shoes. He had changed leagues and the peer pressure changed. That is what drove his espionage.

Henry Lindgren in his classic book, The Psychology of Money, quotes several studies showing the relationship between money and happiness. Money has a substantially positive impact on happiness up to and including the point where one has enough money to pay bills, take a modest vacation and have some money left over for an emergency.

At this point money ceases to be a pressure and this, as I can tell you from personal experience, is highly conducive to happiness. As income increases, however, the happiness quotient does not. Substantial increased increments of income have little effect on increasing happiness levels. [90]

Moreover, there is a strong relativity in happiness related to money. An individual in an environment where the top salary is $75,000 per annum making that amount tends to be happier than another worker earning $100,000 in a different environment where the average salary is $150,000. [91] This is two things: highly counterintuitive and true. Shouldn't an individual earning $100,000 be happier than one earning $75,000? It would be the case-- save the relativity of wages theory expounded by Lindgren.

This can be seen clearly in the Bernie Madoff case. Madoff's son Mark asked him for a loan to buy a home. Of course, the son of a billionaire does not need to go to a bank for a mortgage; he goes to dad. The following quote from the best book on the subject is enlightening.

But to refuse Mark would be almost impossible. How could he explain it after all these years of being the family's bank? His two sons live the way the heirs of any successful hedge fund manager would expect to live......How could he explain it just wasn't a good time to part with a mere six million? [92]

In other words, Bernie Madoff lived entirely in a sub-culture of elite super-rich people. His peer group was all millionaires hence his peer pressure was to provide a loan of a "mere' 6 million. While this may sound silly to all us non-millionaires, it was routine for Bernie Madoff.

Skeptical? An upper middle class person, or even a middle/middle class

---

90 Lindgren, H, The Psychology of Money,
91 Ibid,
92 Henriques, Diana (2011) *The Wizard of Lies*, Holt, NY, P 278

person might be embarrassed if he/she could not afford college tuition for a son/daughter. Try saying to a poor person that a parent was embarrassed because he couldn't afford $50,000 per year for tuition. To that poor person, you are a greedy Bernie Madoff. Peer pressure, particularly money peer pressure emanates from the immediate environment one lives in, not from an overall perspective. [93]

Unfortunately, this notion of money relativity seems to be driven by envy. We humans seem to always notice what the next person above us has and it drives us forward. Often this is a net plus—we are driven to work harder and to achieve more. Conversely it sometimes blinds us and pushes us to places that are not helpful.

We see this envy instinct in the current discussion of income inequality. A successful society needs relatively equal opportunity which will result in winners and losers. As long as the rules are fair and everyone has something approaching equal opportunity we should accept the idea that some people work harder than others, have more talent in a given area and/or accept greater risks than others. Sometimes the acceptance of risk will result in great wealth (Steve Jobs, Bill Gates) and sometimes it results in bankruptcy. No one should begrudge LeBron James and other NBA stars their wealth; they have a unique level of talent and they worked hard to develop it. Taking money away from them will not help to make incomes more equal but it satisfies the envy drive.

Another factor driving money related behavior is the psychological need for excitation. Having, attaining and collecting money can be very exciting. Who hasn't felt a tinge of excitement in receiving a big raise, winning a wager or doubling an investment? Almost no one plays cards without betting—even if the money is nowhere close to making a difference to the player. Nobody goes to the track and does not place a bet on a horse. Gamblers often become compulsive gamblers because

---

93 Thompson, T, (2015) *Common Sense Psychology*, America Star Books, Baltimore, P 110

of the **action** associated with winning and losing. Our present culture places enormous emphasis on safety, both physical and emotional and hence the opportunities for excitation are minimized. This is one reason why the U.S currently has over three million problem gamblers. They seek excitation in a culture saturated with safety. [94]

When adjudicating financial cases PS personnel must keep these psychic nuances in mind. In terms of debt, the circumstances of accrual are critical. Did the subject intentionally spend well beyond her needs on superficial, non-essential goods or did a health crisis and extended hospitalization create a mountain of debt? Were school loans at the root of debt accumulation or was it extravagant vacations? Is debt a long term PATTERN or a one-time event driven by a company cutback and subsequent loss of one's job? Has the individual developed a plan to repay debtors or has he simply declared bankruptcy and walked away? As with all behaviors, the context and proportionality are essential for objective evaluation.

When adjudicating unexplained affluence it is a question of ascertaining a reasonable explanation for a relatively quick change in spending, debt and/or investment posture. Has the subject inherited a sizable amount of money, has he made a successful investment or did he win the lottery. Conversely, has he become a drug runner or a spy? Most often, but not always, unexplained affluence becomes explained with a reasonable investigation.

In the national security arena we have a default position favoring the government i.e. if a case seems too uncertain and critical pieces of a subject's background cannot be confirmed (for example overseas activity) the clearance request should be denied. My own experience has been that this position has been minimal in practice. It seems to violate the visceral fairness rule in that the subject may have spent

---

[94] Shaffer, H, Hall, M, Vander Bilt, J, (September 1999). "Estimating the Prevalence of Disordered Gambling Behavior in the United States and Canada: A Research Synthesis". American Journal of Public Health. 89 (9): 1369–1377.

much time overseas but it is not his fault that certain elements of his residence cannot be confirmed. Hence, in the real world, the opposite assumption may prevail.

In private firms not in the purview of national security, officials may want to carefully examine this predisposition. For example a previous act of violence may have not been prosecuted or pursued or it may have resulted in a No Contest plea (where guilt is not admitted) yet default to denial may be reasonable for a police officer candidate. A reasonable sense of proportion may suggest that a day care provider may shy away from hiring anyone remotely tainted by charges of child molestation. A person with poor financial management skills who we might readily hire as a child care worker might not be hired as a financial counselor. The basic assumption here is that the PS screener need not **prove** a person is unfit but significant ambiguity may push the dial toward denial in some cases.

This predisposition is based on the notion that a security clearance or a job is not a fundamental right granted by the constitution. As previously indicated, too often the public conflates legal protections in criminal cases which should be a high bar indeed, with protections in employment cases. The two are not analogous because in criminal cases one's freedom may be at stake while in employment cases only a job is on the line. Clearly we need severe protection for those charged with crimes that do not apply to job/clearance applicants.

I bring this up now because finances can generate much ambiguity and adjudicative determinations are often far from black and white. A subject's financial status is usually fluid throughout life with a normal upward trajectory in income as the younger person ages. This income increase usually results in different spending patterns and can change the complexion of adjudicative decisions.

In addition, money management can speak to one's capacity for self- restraint. Overspending is a powerful temptation in that it offers huge and immediate rewards for the **absence** of restraint. It is most revealing in cases where need is not the issue but want is the driving force. Our consumer culture is a strong force propelling consumers to buy, buy, buy which is good for the economy but, in many cases, not good for the purchaser.

In summary, financial considerations are the most frequent cause of clearance denial-- but are often accompanied by other contributing case facts in other adjudicative areas. We are a nation saturated in credit. While credit is crucial to a healthy economy, it must be carefully managed on both the micro and macro level. Individuals who are careless in managing their credit may quickly find themselves with a mountain of unsustainable debt. A nation that does not manage it debt appropriately may find itself in the midst of a severe recession—as occurred in the U.S. in 2008. Those challenges sometimes generate very high interest payments which can result in high levels of debt generating a significant vulnerability. The spy Brian Regan had about $120,000 in credit card debt at the time he decided to commit espionage. [95] This was the primary motivational factor in his decision and he felt he had no way out—other than espionage. Wise adjudicative decisions in the area of finances are crucial to a healthy PS screening program.

---

95 Affidavit, U.S. District Court, Alexandria VA, 2002

CHAPTER TEN

OTHER ADJUDICATIVE ISSUES

I devoted a chapter each to substance use/abuse and finances because they are the most commonly encountered issues in the PS field. Some of the remaining adjudicative guidelines need some amplification but none require a full chapter. Ergo I will address several of these guidelines in the space of this chapter—starting with crime.

Most of us think of street crime when the notion of criminal behavior is introduced. In PS we evaluate white collar crime just as aggressively as street crime. White collar crime costs the economy much more than street crime; the single case of Bernie Madoff accounted for upwards of 60 billion dollars' worth of theft/embezzlement. Most street thefts/robberies net less than $50.00.

Obviously violent crime is the top priority and accounts for about 52% of the current federal and state prison population. (Contrary to popular belief only 16% of state and federal prisoners are incarcerated for drug crimes.) [96] As with most behaviors, recency is an important consideration. The more recent the behavior the more likely is

---

[96] Lopez, G, Why you can't blame mass incarceration on the war on drugs, Vox, 30 May 2017, Retrieved 7 Nov 2019, https://www.vox.com/policy-and-politics/2017/5/30/15591700/mass-incarceration-john-pfaff-locked-in

the possibility of denial. Context is equally important; in cases where there is an arrest, investigators should interview law enforcement officers whenever possible. This is particularly important because a law enforcement officer can often provide context.

(Conversely, many law enforcement agencies deny access to criminal records and police/court personnel because the investigators represent non-law enforcement agencies. This was the case in the Aaron Alexis case wherein Seattle PD routinely denied information to government investigators resulting in a deadly mass shooting. Some police departments are reconsidering this policy—as well they should.)

Prosecuting attorneys are notorious for overcharging; what is really petty assault is frequently charged as felonious assault so that the person charged will have an incentive to plea bargain. On the other hand, what is sometimes labeled assault 2nd degree is sometimes pled down to common harassment. Hence the need for context and a genuine explanation is important. The crime may not be as ominous as the charge appears or it may be considerably worse than the outcome suggests.

Age is an important factor when considering criminal behavior. Most crime is committed by males and males ages 14 to 34 account for a disproportionate amount of all crime. As that demographic grows it usually presages an increase in crime. Hence PS professionals should take that datum into account.

Crime is an area where past behavior is particularly predictive of future behavior. This is especially so with serious crimes. Released prisoners with the highest re-arrest rates are Robbers (70.2%), Burglars (74.0%), Larcenists (74.6%), Motor vehicle thieves (78.8%), those possessing or selling stolen property (77.4%), those possessing, using, or selling illegal weapons (70.2%). [97] These individuals, especially those ages 14 to 34

---

97 Adjudicator Desk Reference, 2007 statistics, PERSEREC, P 49, Retrieved 12 Nov, 2019,

represent high risk for jobs and/or clearances. Of course this judgment should be made with consideration of context and mitigating factors—if any are present.

It is also important to note that most crimes are NOT reported. Only 39% of crimes are reported to the police and only 20% of those lead to an arrest. In addition only 73% of those arrested are prosecuted.[98] These data illustrate that the criminal has the law of averages on his side; he probably will not get apprehended, if apprehended, he may not be prosecuted and if prosecuted he may not be convicted. These data call out for use of polygraph in PS screening. Chances are almost nil that someone will admit to crime where there was no apprehension was made and/or no record exists. Government agencies which do not employ polygraph are at a distinct disadvantage in the all-important area of criminal behavior.

My final point on crime may be obvious. Someone who is willing to break the law in a relatively serious matter (felony or misdemeanor) may tell us a great deal about that person. A subject who risks disgrace, possible jail time and loss of income/ employment is certainly taking a very substantial risk. She is also displaying very poor judgment and discretion and such actions speak to overall trustworthiness and reliability.

Here we must make a distinction between volitional crime and impulsive, extemporaneous crime. Volitional crime is an engaged choice—something that is premeditated and considered in advance. The individual thinks about the act beforehand and plans the act. There is no spontaneity. Almost all white collar crime falls into this category and, since it is planned and not subject to impulse, should be taken more seriously than it generally is. In a calm, rational moment

---

https://www.dhra.mil/portals/52/documents/perserec/adr_version_4.pdf
98 Bureau of Justice Statistics. (2001). Nature and distribution of known offenses. In Sourcebook of Criminal Justice Statistics, 2001. Washington, DC: U.S. Department of Justice.

this person has **decided** to break the law and assume the accompanying risk. Insurance fraud, a common white collar crime, falls into this category.

Much street crime falls into the opposite category i.e. it is often the result of some spontaneous turn of events. In my own experience as a police officer in the South Bronx the most common type of assault occurred between two inebriated males in a bar. This mode far outstripped pre-planned assaults which were usually accompanied by a robbery/rape effort. Obviously the violent nature of the latter crime takes on greater significance while the former type of assault is more readily mitigated. The basic point here is that premeditation of any crime adds considerable negative impact and is more difficult to mitigate.

Let me now turn to allegiance.

Allegiance can be credibly described as the most important element of a national security investigation. Without loyalty to the nation all other adjudicative matters sink to irrelevance. It is the least frequent area confronted by the PS professional but arguably the most important. Hence I choose to single it out for discussion. It may be analogous to a nuclear power plant accident; they occur very infrequently but because of the potential severity great care should be taken to minimize vulnerability. Normally this issue would be a no-brainer with no need for any further comment—but the world is changing.

As a part of a national security investigation the following questions are asked of all sources: *Is subject a loyal American citizen? Do you know of any reason to question subject's loyalty to the U.S?* I myself did more than 5,000 such interviews in the late 70s and never once received a negative answer.

Today, however, only 49% of Millennials describe themselves as patriotic.[99] This dynamic drastically changes the emphasis and focus on the issue of allegiance. Although allegiance is largely a state of mind we must nonetheless try to make judgments based primarily on conduct such as membership in radical groups, advocating the overthrow of the government, financial contributions to radical groups or participation in certain hate crimes. These behaviors may inform us as to a person's allegiance.

It must be said that in our polyglot world the entire notion of national loyalty seems to be diminishing. In defense of Millenials, it is not the case that they demonstrate a loyalty to another nation; they do not. Rather, many are somewhat indifferent to **any** national loyalty. Moreover, in my opinion, the depth of national loyalty in the overall population seems to be diminishing as well. That is, those who profess an allegiance to a nation seem to have lesser conviction underlying that allegiance. This makes the critical job of evaluating allegiance much more difficult.

In the corporate, non-national security world, allegiance may be a different type of issue. There is no handling of classified information hence no threat of potential damage to the national security is manifest. Nonetheless corporations need to be wary of economic espionage-- in which the Chinese are very aggressive. In the case of hiring a foreign citizen with the appropriate visa-- that citizen's loyalty is almost always to his own country. Ergo, if the Chinese government asked him to report on proprietary matters he might be inclined to do so. In the case of a U.S. citizen working in China being asked by the U.S. government to provide proprietary information, one has to conclude that citizen would be more likely to provide that information to his own government. So too would a Chinese citizen. Consequently, corporations need to remain cognizant of this possible vulnerability.

---

99 Pew Research, Social & Demographic Trends, *Millennials in Adulthood*, 7 March 2014, Retrieved 13 Nov 2019, https://www.pewsocialtrends.org/2014/03/07/millennials-in-adulthood/

In short, the adjudicative guideline covering allegiance makes a categorical, non-caveated statement: *An individual must be of unquestionable allegiance to the United States.*[100] In national security cases where allegiance is ambiguous the default position should be denial. A bad adjudicative decision based on drug use, finances, crime etc. does not come with the same degree of risk as that of allegiance. In essence, we simply cannot afford to be wrong on the issue of allegiance.

Misuse of information technology systems is another critical area of PS inquiry. Spies like Bob Hanssen and mass leakers such as Chelsea Manning and Edward Snowden all used IT skills and systems to facilitate their actions. Brian Regan collected most of his classified information via Intellink and planned to sell it to the Iraqis for 13 million.[101] IT capacities, as miraculous as they are in terms of productivity, make us much more vulnerable to wrongdoing because the access most cleared persons have is enormous.

Back in the 60s and 70s, before IT systems were ubiquitous, the access of the average intelligence officer was minimal. When the writer first joined the IC I had a two-draw file cabinet with perhaps 30 files—fifteen of which were unclassified. Aside from some tidbit I may have picked up at a meeting this was the sum total of my access. Had I decided to walk into the Soviet Embassy I would have had a very small volume of sensitive information and consequently the damage I might have caused would have been limited.

Not so today. Post 911, at the suggestion of the 911 Commission, IC made a concerted effort to share more information. The **need to know principle** (sharing classified information only with those cleared individuals who required it for their duties) was subordinated

---

100 Center for the Development of Security Excellence, Job Aid 13: Adjudicative Guidelines, April 2015. Retrieved, 14 Nov 2019, https://www.cdse.edu/documents/cdse/job-aid-13-adjudicative-guidelines-v2.pdf

101 Affidavit, United States versus Brian Regan, U.S. District Court in Virginia, Para 20, Aug 2001, Retrieved 16 Nov 2019, https://fas.org/irp/ops/ci/regan_complaint.html

to the **must share principle**.¹⁰² Some formerly discrete databases were connected and access for those with minimal need to know was enhanced. As a result of the enhanced human access and better connected databases the amount of information available to a wrongdoer is enormous. For example, Chelsea Manning, an army sergeant at an obscure military base in Iraq, released over 750,000 sensitive/classified documents she had electronic access to. ¹⁰³ Thirty-five years ago Chelsea Manning would have had access to a very small fraction of that data.

Hence mishandling of IT systems must take a high priority in the PS world. A classic instance of IT misuse is the case of former Director of Central Intelligence (DCI) John Deutch. Deutch was DCI in the Clinton administration and during his tenure, he used several unclassified computers to store classified information at his residence. This was clearly against regulations and two hard drives containing a large volume of classified information (and connected to the Internet) were vulnerable to exposure. The material subject to possible exposure included Top Secret Code word information—among the most sensitive in all of government. ¹⁰⁴ After a lengthy investigation leaving no doubt as to his culpability, Deutch planned to plead guilty to mishandling government secrets. He was, however, preemptively pardoned by President Bill Clinton just before he (Clinton) left office. His security clearance was revoked in 1999 by then DCI George Tenet. ¹⁰⁵

The investigation could not determine if any government secrets had been accessed via the Internet connection, but the risk was high. I can tell you from my own experience that Deutch came to CIA with

---

102 This is not to suggest that the need to know principle has been abandoned. It has not but it certainly has been de-emphasized.
103 Chelsea Manning, WIKIPEDIA, Retrieved 14 Nov 2019
104 CIA Inspector General Report, Snider, L.B. 18 Feb, 2000, Retrieved, 15 Nov 2019, https://fas.org/irp/cia/product/ig_deutch.html
105 Sniffen, MJ, *Ex-CIA Head Planned Guilty Plea*, Washington Post, 24 Jan 2001. Retrieved, 15 Nov 2019, http://www.washingtonpost.com/wp-srv/aponline/20010124/aponline163741_000.htm

a reformer's attitude. He had little regard for existing agency personnel or procedures and exhibited more than a hint of Narcissism. His downfall resulted from a common Washington "disorder"-- the arrogance of power. As individuals accrete more power they are increasingly at risk for this disorder. The higher one goes the more one is surrounded by yes people who laugh at one's jokes, nod approvingly at innocuous statements and defer to one's presence. In return the sycophants receive access to power and, often, promotion. This is a very common, but certainly not universal, syndrome in the halls of Washington. This is not a blanket indictment; I dare say, that most, but not all, people in Washington achieve in accordance with their abilities and work ethic, not by sycophancy.

Deutch's misuse of IT systems was intentional, blatant and arrogant. The lesson for the PS professional is that powerful people often incorporate the notion that the rules apply to you but do not apply to them. Often, powerful people are not scrutinized as aggressively as they should be because whoever uncovers wrongdoing on the part of the powerful now has a huge problem which could well be a career ender. This is an unfortunate state of affairs that the PS officer is at odds with. In the Deutch case his wrongdoing was uncovered **after** his departure from CIA.

IT misuse often suggests the subject may have a problem with rules and regulations in general. This is particularly important in that true anonymity, and sometimes perceived anonymity, may embolden individuals to engage in cyber wrongdoing. Cyber investigations can be very complex and most experts believe that substantial amounts of cyber-crime go undetected and many that are detected the perpetrator of the offense cannot be identified. Consequently, PS officials must rely more on a person's conscience, perhaps cyber-conscience is a more descriptive term, as compared to his perception of apprehension which is diminished in the cyber world.

The scale of the potential IT problem is breathtaking. Baltimore was recently the victim of a ransomware attack in which the perpetrators shut down most of the city's electronic infrastructure. The city did not pay the ransom but it nonetheless cost the city 18.2 million in lost or delayed revenues and IT replacement costs to insure no such attack could occur in the future. [106] The cyber-criminals were never apprehended. Some private companies, under threat of perhaps going out of business, have paid ransom to have their systems restored. One can only imagine the horror if some insider in the national security world engineered a ransomware attack against agencies like CIA, FBI or NSA. This amply demonstrates the need for good PS screening of our cyber specialists. The losses that even one insider can accomplish are unimaginable.

The adjudicative guidelines include the category of sexual behavior. I choose to address this category not because it is a frequent issue in personnel security but because it is highly impactful when the issue arises. I also will expand the definition to sex and loving which I will label mating. The intent of the adjudicative guideline is clearly not limited to sexual activity per se but meant to include the entire package of attraction, romance and the entirety of the mating endeavor. I am addressing this separately not because PS professionals encounter this issue directly; rather they most often encounter it indirectly.

I am certain the reader knows at least one individual who ruined his life over a mating relationship gone badly. The psychological and emotional allure of mating, consciously or unconsciously, drives much of our behavior. There are no stronger feelings, save survival, than romantic attraction. It is almost narcotic-like in its effect on the brain. Someone involved in new love has an extraordinary amount of serotonin activity in the brain. In one simple phrase—it feels great to be newly in love.

---

106 Duncan, I, Baltimore Sun, *Baltimore estimates cost of ransomware attack at $18.2 million as government begins to restore email accounts,* 29 May 2019, Retrieved 16 Nov 2019, https://www.baltimoresun.com/maryland/baltimore-city/bs-md-ci-ransomware-email-20190529-story.html

In his book, *How to Fix a Broken Heart*, Guy Winch, Ph.D. discusses a case of a woman who had a diagnosis of breast cancer in her right breast, went through the entire treatment protocols, got well and then got a diagnosis in her left breast and went through treatment again. It took her about three months to recover, physically and emotionally from the ordeal. She was subsequently engaged and her fiancée ended the relationship. A year later she had not recovered from the emotional loss.[107] That is a perfect example of how powerful the business of mating is.

The previously described tension between comprehensiveness and invasiveness is particularly germane in the area of sexuality. After all, sexual behavior is the most private of all activities and-- do PS personnel really need to delve into this? Would it not be better to yield comprehensiveness to avoid invasiveness?

No, it would not.

The previously described case of the astronaut Lisa, Nowick perfectly illustrates the power of mating. She had it ALL—husband, children, lucrative career and promising future but threw it away on a fling. Want more evidence?

Vitaly Yurchenko was a high level intelligence official with the Soviet Union who defected to the United States in 1985-- leaving behind a wife and family. He supplied CIA with two names of intelligence operatives who were secretly working for the KGB, Edward Howard and Ronald Pelton. Yurchenko requested his name not be released to the media but it nonetheless leaked. After a brief orientation period in the U.S. Yurchenko requested he be transported to Canada to be reunited with a former extramarital lover. This was accomplished but he was spurned by the woman. Shortly thereafter Yurchenko re-defected back to the

---

[107] Winch, G, (2018) How to Fix Broken Heart, Simon & Schuster, NY.

Soviet Union claiming he had been captured and drugged by the CIA. [108]

At the time much discussion (mostly uninformed media) generated a theory that Yurchenko was a false defector intentionally sent to mislead U.S. intelligence. I will not explore the entire debate; suffice to say that theory is patently absurd. Yurchenko was a legitimate defector who changed his mind after being scorned by his former lover.

This case also speaks to the power of love/mating. Here was an individual who undoubtedly was in the top ten percent in terms of money, power and status in the USSR but he threw it all away in remembrance of an affair and the hope of a rekindling of that affair. He was no love struck teenager but a mature male with all the accoutrements of stability and success.

The cases of Lisa Nowick and Vitaly Yurchenko amply illustrate why PS professionals should screen for sexual/mating behavior issues. Neither had any psychological disorders but those feelings of love/lust/romance can overpower even the most emotionally stable individuals. Look at a partial list of some of our leaders who risked it all for love/lust: Senator Larry Craig, Governor Mark Sanford, Senator (and vice presidential candidate) John Edwards, Congressman Anthony Weiner and President Bill Clinton. These are people who had virtually everything this life had to offer: power, money, fame and status yet they risked it all for this magical thing call love/lust. This is why PS officers need to scrutinize sexual behavior, when appropriate.

Let me state early on in this discussion that sexual behavior that is between two adults that is consensual, private and discreet comes with a strong predisposition toward acceptance. Basically, what is done by two adults in their own bedroom is largely outside the scope of PS screening. (I will get to the "largely" part later.)

---

108 Kalugin, O, Former Soviet KGB Officer, Texas A & M conference, 1999.

To add additional context, PS professionals get an infinitesimal amount of sexual information. That information is derived from three sources: polygraph (not used by all agencies) criminal records and/or subject interviews. Polygraphs in the IC NO LONGER ask a question about sex; rather the questions on crime and misuse of a government computer (viewing porn on government time) will sometimes instigate discussions on sexual behaviors. In addition, the IC NO LONGER screens for or denies a security clearance based on same sex attraction/behavior. Despite the fact that information collected on sexual activities is very infrequent, PS officers still need to know how to handle it when encountered.

The relevant security question pertinent to sex/mating issues is about the same as other PS issues i.e. is this behavior a harmless idiosyncrasy or is it reflective of a larger psychological problem. Unusual sexual behaviors, not otherwise defined as paraphilias, in and of themselves are not areas of concern. Activities such as swinging, certain fetishes and extramarital affairs are unusual but not abnormal, deviant or illegal. They may merit some minimal degree of scrutiny but are not **necessarily** disqualifying. If such behaviors bleed over into the criminal arena they should be evaluated as such.

Sexual behavior in the national security world has overwhelmingly been coupled with the threat of coercion. The culture at large is saturated with sex and simply loves a good sex/espionage tale. Unfortunately for those who enjoy these James Bond like exploits, the real world has had very few of these entertaining incidences. One expansive study of espionage examining 173 spy cases since 1947 found that between 1980 and 2007 there were zero cases of espionage committed by trusted insiders as a result of sexual coercion. That same study found only 13 cases of coercion from 1947 to 1979.[109] Coercive espionage appears

---

[109] Herbig, K, PERSEREC, *Changes in Espionage by Americans: 1947-2007*, March 2008. P 31, Retrieved 17 Nov, 2019. https://www.dhra.mil/Portals/52/Documents/perserec/tr08-05.pdf

to be a thing of the past—or at least a rare event in today's world.

This is quite reasonable because to recruit an asset based on blackmail is to recruit a very angry, resentful and revenge-driven person. A case officer needs genuine cooperation in providing legitimate sensitive information and cases based on blackmail are much more likely to result in minimization, obfuscation and subtle, perhaps imperceptible, resistance. Coercion is a very bad way of doing business and most intelligence agencies throughout the world recognize this. Consequently there is very little sexual coercion in the espionage game.[110] Unfortunately, intelligence community personnel who ought to know better still pervade our rules and regulations with this underlying assumption—including the adjudicative guidelines I have been quoting throughout this book.

This is not to say that coercion and blackmail **never** occur; on occasion they do but the policy makers in the IC grossly overstate and over-apply this notion to the point of claiming blackmail potential in some behaviors that are clearly not susceptible. It is not the case that we should eliminate coercion and blackmail from our vernacular; rather we should place those possibilities in perspective i.e. they are rare and should not pervade and dominate our thinking and actions.

Let me offer an example of the difficulty in basing rules on potential coercion. Let's say we have a married couple who are both intelligence officers—a common scenario today. They take a vacation overseas and the opposition intelligence service learns of their plans. The service then prepares their hotel with surveillance equipment and films them making love. The service then approaches them and threatens to release the videos on the Internet unless they provide classified information. Do we forbid our married couples from having sex overseas? Is this an inherent vulnerability that we need to evaluate? Aren't

---

[110] Charney, D & Ervin, J, The Psychology of Espionage, The Intelligencer, Vol 22 No. 1, Spring 2016, P 4.

they subject to sexual blackmail? I will let the reader draw her own conclusions.

The adjudicative guideline should focus largely, but not exclusively, on paraphilias i.e. sexual disorders. The definition of a paraphilia is: *a sexual desire or behavior that involves another person's psychological distress, injury or death, or a desire for sexual behaviors involving unwilling persons or persons unable to give legal consent for a period of six months or more. One must feel personal distress about their interest, not merely distress resulting from society's disapproval. It must be obligatory i.e. result in dysfunction, require participation of non-consenting individuals, lead to legal complications, interfere with social relationships.* [111]

While I might quibble with this definition the important point for the PS professional is that if a behavior can be categorized as a paraphilia, there should be a default toward disapproval. The presence of a paraphilia, by definition, suggests a mental health imbalance that is NOT a harmless idiosyncrasy but symptomatic of a disordered psyche.

Some would argue this point. In the case of sado-masochism we may have two consenting adults engaging in this practice in the privacy of their own home. This should meet the aforementioned test of two consenting and discreet adults in the privacy of their own home—should it not?

No, it should not. The notion of inflicting pain, real or simulated, on another human being, consenting or not, strikes me as disordered. Likewise, receipt of pain is equally suggestive of psychological malfunction. It is not a healthy mind/psyche that gets sexual thrills from inflicting or receiving pain. Call me a prude.

Returning to my original point, an adjudicator is on firm ground denying in cases where a paraphilia is present. Of course, the case has much

---

[111] DSM V, P 566

more credibility if a clinician makes a diagnosis but, in the absence of a mental health professional, a non-clinical judgment can be made on the basis of the behavior alone.

This is not to suggest that this judgment is **automatic** in these cases. It is not. Mitigating factors such as adolescent activities or very dated behavior may contraindicate denial. As always, the adjudicator must take into account the overall context and proportionality of the activity and make a decision based on the Whole Person Concept.

It is also important to point out that the DSM V does NOT include so called sexual addiction or porn addiction. These labels are products of psychologists and psychiatrist who treat clients for behavioral sexual issues that create difficulty for their patients. This is as it should be; people may need lots of help managing their sex/love drive but that does not necessarily translate into the much overused term of addiction. At the time of this writing the World Health Organization has recognized sexual problems as addictions but the U.S. mental health community has not.[112] Of course some of those U.S. members are clamoring for recognition of some sexual behavior as addictions but the DSM committee has thus far resisted. Let me offer an editorial comment.

One can only imagine the exploitation that defense counselors would engage in use of sexual addiction as a legal defense. In the real world, addiction or no addiction, one is responsible for one's own behavior. This **could** still be held true in the legal world—but I have my doubts. In the larger culture, where potential jurors live, the term addiction has become almost synonymous with victimhood. One almost never hears in the mainstream media of culpability for one's own addiction. You will hear it here. Addiction is not an overnight phenomenon; rather it is almost always a gradual downward, high risk trend in using

---

[112] Leipholtz, B, The Fix, *World Health Organization Adds Sex Addiction to Disease List*, 17 July, 2018, Retrieved 19 Nov 2019. https://www.thefix.com/world-health-organization-adds-sex-addiction-disease-list

substances. Most addicts are 100% responsible for their addiction—and for their recovery.

In any event, the parallel with sexual behavior is inapt. Of course there are lots of hormones involved in sexual arousal and activity and these hormones affect the brain. This is a near universal experience with all of us; we desire sex/loving and our brain chemistry drives us. Some of us do not manage our sex drive well and wind up negatively affecting our lives. If this is the definition of addiction, then a very high number of the population are sex addicts. Who hasn't negatively affected their lives in pursuit of love?

While the PS community should focus primarily on paraphilias they should not do so exclusively. A psychologist familiar with the Lisa Nowick case stated she had no disorder; she was merely overcome by the strength of love and subsequent jealousy. The spy cases of Richard Miller (FBI), Sharon Scranage (CIA) and Clayton Lonetree (USMC) were cases of love/lust but none of these individuals had a paraphilia (nor were they blackmailed.) It is reasonable to conclude that "normal" love/mating behavior projects more risk than disordered behavior. This is yet another reason that PS should scrutinize sex/love based behavior---within reasonable limits.

Sexual behavior, although uncommonly encountered in the PS, world can be highly impactful. Our sexual/mating instincts, consciously or unconsciously, can affect our behavior significantly. Previously quoted cases are simply a very small sample of a larger population who negatively affect their lives in the love game. Given the potential for invasiveness in scrutinizing mating activities, the PS professional is faced with a bureaucratically perilous conundrum. Nonetheless, the issue cannot be ignored.

CHAPTER ELEVEN

SUMMARY AND CONCLUSIONS

Personnel Security is the imperfect art/science of attempting to predict future behavior by scrutinizing past behavior. This is done via the Whole Person Concept which is defined as evaluating a person's entire behavioral profile-- the negative behaviors accompanied by mitigating factors. A sense of proportionality and context are critical to making good decisions and provide decisional boundaries. In the event of the presence of marginal or inadequately descriptive data, the default position in national security cases is denial. The attainment of a security clearance or a job is not a constitutional right and conflation with protections in criminal cases is misguided.

There are 13 adjudicative guidelines constructed by the Intelligence Community which provide the roadmap for PS implementation. (Appendix) The core of implementation consists of application submission, data collection (investigation and/or polygraph including a subject interview) adjudication and periodic reinvestigations. Most, but not all, of these guidelines can be applied to the non-national security cases and provide a basic blueprint.

The degree and intensity of the PS effort can and does vary. Today there are a myriad of online background investigations, most of which are minimal and consist largely of searches of publically available databases. A core decision a corporation must make is-- what degree of PS scrutiny do they want and/or can afford. In today's litigious world companies are increasingly afraid of liability for the actions of rogue employees.

The national security arena is also moving toward existing database reviews (Continuous Evaluation, CE) as a vital part of the PS effort. It is important to note that there are reliable databases in certain areas (crime, finances) and no databases in other areas (allegiance, sexual behavior, illegal drug use, misuse of information technology, personal conduct.) There is currently a large backlog of government cases and hence the pressure to use electronic database checks in lieu of reinvestigations is high. As a temporary measure this makes a great deal of sense but as a permanent alternative to, or as an excuse to minimize the reinvestigation effort may be suicidal. The only source that can provide useful information on allegiance, drug use, sexual behavior, misuse of information technology and other areas of concern is a person. Personal investigative contact is the most expensive source of information but must nevertheless be retained.

After many years of ambivalence the IC and the corporate world has seemed to settle on the notion that the insider threat is the greater risk than the initial applicant. I have emphasized in this book that most insiders came to employment/clearance with little to no risk factors but life changed that. In espionage cases this pattern may be tilting slightly towards recruitment by a foreign service but it nonetheless remains the case that the majority of the threat is the insider. In the period 1947-2007, spies volunteered at a rate of 60% as compared to recruitment by a foreign service which was 40%.[113] Divorce, financial problems, mental health issues, illness and/or substances use/abuse issues can convert a person from low risk to high risk. This is why it is critical to retain an active reinvestigation program which incorporates

---

113 Herbig, P 25

human sources as well as electronic sources. To de-emphasize reinvestigation is to change the focus from a greater threat (insider) to a lesser threat (outsider.)

Having been in the field for 40 years, I note that we seem to be in an everlasting state of reform. After the Edward Snowden case, reinvestigation efforts were intensified. This caused, in part, the development of a large backlog, approximately 700,000 in a population of over 4 million. Ergo, the emphasis today is to reduce the backlog by loosening investigative standards. The next time a big insider case breaks we undoubtedly will look around and blame someone for prioritizing backlog reduction over quality reinvestigation. And on and on it goes.

Rather than remain in a constant state of ostensible reform we need to do something that we Americans are perfectly awful at—recognizing limits. This starts with recognizing that the PS screening in some cases was just fine but the person developed issues after the fact. I have stated this several times in this book but it bears repeating—not every case with a bad ending is a badly executed case. Yes, we should do a serious post mortem and perhaps we should make some changes but most of the time the system did not fail—the individual did. In our rush to hold someone, anyone, accountable we too often engage in scapegoating. Conversely, if it is clear that substantial individual negligence occurred in a given case those employees should be dealt with firmly.

The one area that could substantially improve the quality and quantity of the PS process is a greater reliance on polygraph rather than the background investigation. Polygraph is less expensive, less time consuming, produces more information and that information is more reliable. For too long emotional, non-thinking has dominated these discussions and for once we need to have an adult conversation. We are living in a time of exorbitant narcissism where unpopularity is about the worst sin one can commit. We must get past this.

There was a time when most agencies had their own employees performing background investigations. The reinventing government effort moved that dial toward contractor use. I am not certain if that was a wise, productive change or not and I do not think anyone else knows either. Hence, the PS community should launch a research project to address that issue.

Inside the government PS community, we need to stop employing the default position of approving a clearance in the absence of confirmatory information. Too many in the PS field believe and act like one is indeed entitled to a clearance unless the government can prove otherwise. The opposite presupposition is correct and should be applied.

Next, do NOT let periodic reinvestigations fall behind; the government needs to spend the money to get it done but simply does not want to do that. Do it.

All PS programs should have an aperiodic piece. Yes, the reinvestigation cycle should be either a five or ten year cycle but reinvestigation at irregular intervals should also be an integral part of the program. This can be done with a very small part of the population so it costs very little. In order to maximize the deterrent effect, it should be made very clear to the population that an aperiodic program is in effect. The advantage of this practice is it does not allow wrongdoers, like Edward Snowden, to plan their activities around a five year reinvestigation cycle. He knew he had five years to accomplish what he wanted and planned accordingly. Aperiodic reinvestigations can create a substantial deterrent at very little cost.

Personnel Security deals with the most complex of dynamics—human behavior. It does not lend itself to formulaic thinking but relies on human judgment. A good program, while costly, may help to insure a better quality employee and minimize the risks of large lawsuits. Programs, of necessity, vary in scale and intensity depending on what is to be protected.

Personnel Security cannot guarantee that untoward events will not occur—nobody can do that. What good PS does do, is reduce the risk that unfit people will be employed and thereby reduce the risk of insider wrongdoing.

APPENDIX

AJUDICATIVE GUIDELINES

The 13 Adjudicative Guidelines

Guideline A – Allegiance to the U.S.

Concern: An individual must be of unquestionable allegiance to the United States. The willingness to safeguard classified information is in doubt if there is any reason to suspect an individual's allegiance to the United States.

Disqualifying Conditions (a) Involvement in, training to commit, support of, or advocacy of any act of: Sabotage, Espionage , Treason , Terrorism , Sedition (b) Association or sympathy with individuals attempting to commit, or who are committing any of the above acts (c) Association or sympathy with individuals or organizations that advocate, threaten, or use force or violence or any other illegal unconstitutional means to: Overthrow or influence Federal, state or local government, Prevent

Federal, state, or local government personnel from performing their duties, Gain retribution for perceived wrongs caused by the Federal, state, or local government, Prevent others from exercising their rights under the Constitutional or laws of the U.S. or of any state.

Mitigating Conditions: (a) Unaware of unlawful aims of the individual or organization and severed ties upon learning (b) Only involved with the lawful or humanitarian aspects of such an organization (c) Only involved for a short time, and was attributable to curiosity or academic interest (d) Involvement or association with such activities occurred under such unusual circumstances, or so much times has elapsed, that it is unlikely to recur and does not cast doubt on the individual's current reliability, trustworthiness, or loyalty.

Guideline B – Foreign Influence

Concern: Foreign contacts and interests may be a security concern if the individual has divided loyalties or foreign financial interests, may be manipulated or induced to help a foreign person, group, organization, or government in a way that is not in U.S. interests, or is vulnerable to pressure or coercion by any foreign interest. Adjudication under this Guideline can and should consider the identity of the foreign country in which the foreign contact or financial interest is located, including, but not limited to, such considerations as whether the foreign country is known to target United States citizens to obtain protected information and/or is associated with a risk of terrorism.

Disqualifying Conditions: (a) contact with a foreign family member, business or professional associate, friend, or other person who is a citizen of or resident in a foreign country if that contact creates a heightened risk of foreign exploitation, inducement, manipulation, pressure, or coercion (b) connections to a foreign person, group, government, or country that create a potential conflict of interest between the individual's obligation to protect sensitive information or technology and the individual's desire to help a foreign person, group, or country by providing that information (c) counterintelligence information, that may be classified, indicates that the individual's access to protected information may involve unacceptable risk to national security (d) sharing living quarters with a person or persons, regardless of citizenship status, if that relationship creates a heightened risk of foreign inducement, manipulation, pressure, or coercion (e) a substantial business, financial, or property interest in a foreign country, or in any foreign-owned or foreign-operated business, which could subject the individual to heightened risk of foreign influence or exploitation (f) failure to report, when required, association with a foreign national (g) unauthorized association with a suspected or known agent, associate, or employee of a foreign intelligence service (h) indications that representatives or nationals from a foreign country are acting to increase the vulnerability of the individual to possible future exploitation, inducement, manipulation, pressure, or coercion Mitigating Conditions (a) The nature of the relationships with foreign persons, the country in which these persons are located, or the positions or activities of those persons in that country are such that it is unlikely the individual will be placed in a position of having to choose between the interests of a foreign individual, group, organization, or government and the interests of the U.S. (b) There is no conflict of interest due to the individual's sense of loyalty or obligation to the foreign person or entity, or so minimal, or the individual has deep and longstanding relationships and loyalties in the U.S., it is expected that the individual would resolve any conflict of interest in favor of U.S . interests (c) Contact or communication with foreign citizens is so casual and infrequent that there is little likelihood that it could create a risk for foreign influence or exploitation (d) Foreign contacts and activities are on U.S. Government business or are approved by the cognizant security authority (d) The foreign contacts and activities are on U.S. Government business or are approved by the cognizant security authority (e) the individual has promptly complied with existing agency requirements regarding the reporting of contacts, requests, or threats from persons, groups, or organizations from a foreign country Ü (f) the value or routine nature of the foreign business, financial, or property interests is such that they are unlikely to result in a conflict and could not be used effectively to influence, manipulate, or pressure the individual

Guideline C – Foreign Preference

Concern: When an individual acts in such a way as to indicate a preference for a foreign country over the United States, then he or she may be prone to provide information or make decisions that are harmful to the interests of the United States.

Disqualifying Conditions: (a) Exercise of any right, privilege or obligation of foreign citizenship after becoming a U.S. citizen or through the foreign citizenship of a family member. This includes but is not limited to: Possession of a current foreign passport, Foreign military service or willingness to bear arms for a foreign country, Accepting foreign benefits (educational, medical, retirement, social welfare, etc.) Residence in a foreign country to meet citizenship requirements, Using foreign citizenship to protect financial/business interests in another country, Seeking or holding political office in a foreign country, Voting in a foreign election, (b) Action to acquire or obtain recognition of a foreign citizenship by an American citizen, (c) performing or attempting to perform duties, or otherwise acting, so as to serve the interests of a foreign person, group, organization, or government in conflict with the national security interest, (d) any statement or action that shows allegiance to a country other than the United States: for example, declaration of intent to renounce United States citizenship; renunciation of United States citizenship

Mitigating Conditions: (a) Dual citizenship is based solely on parents' citizenship or birth in a foreign country (b) Expressed willingness to renounce dual citizenship (c) Exercise of the rights, privileges, or obligations of foreign citizenship occurred before the individual became a U.S. citizen or when the individual was a minor (d) Use of a foreign passport is approved by the cognizant security authority (e) Passport has been destroyed, surrendered to the cognizant security authority, or otherwise invalidated (f) The vote in a foreign election was encouraged by the U.S. Government

Guideline D – Sexual Behavior

Concern: Sexual behavior that involves a criminal offense indicates a personality or emotional disorder, reflects lack of judgment or discretion, or which may subject the individual to undue influence or coercion, exploitation, or duress can raise questions about an individual's reliability, trustworthiness and ability to protect classified information. No adverse inference concerning the standards in the Guideline may be raised solely on the basis of the sexual orientation of the individual. Some sexual behavior can raise questions about an individual's reliability, trustworthiness, and ability to protect classified information.

Disqualifying Conditions: (a) Sexual behavior of a criminal nature, whether or not the individual has been prosecuted, (b) A pattern of compulsive, self-destructive, or high-risk behavior that the person is unable to stop or that may be or that may be symptomatic of a personality disorder, (c) Sexual behavior that causes vulnerability to coercion, exploitation, or duress, (d) Sexual behavior of a public nature and/or that which reflects lack of discretion or judgment

Mitigating Conditions: (a) Behavior occurred prior to or during adolescence and there is no evidence of subsequent conduct of a similar nature, (b) The sexual behavior happened so long ago, so infrequently, or under such unusual circumstances, that it is unlikely to recur and does not cast doubt on the individual's current reliability, trustworthiness, or good judgment , (c) Behavior no longer serves as a basis for coercion, exploitation, or duress, (d) The sexual behavior is strictly private, consensual, and discreet

Guideline E – Personal Conduct

Concern: Conduct involving questionable judgment, lack of candor, dishonesty, or unwillingness to comply with rules and regulations can raise questions about an individual's reliability, trustworthiness and ability to protect classified information. Of special interest is any failure to provide truthful and candid answers during the security clearance process or any other failure to cooperate with the security clearance process. The following will normally result in an unfavorable clearance action or administrative termination of further processing for clearance eligibility: (a) Refusal, or failure without reasonable cause, to undergo or cooperate with security processing (i.e. meeting with an investigator, completing security forms or releases, cooperating with medical or psychological evaluation) (b) Refusal to provide full, frank and truthful answers to lawful questions of investigators, security officials or other official representatives in connection with a personnel security or trustworthiness determination Disqualifying Conditions: (a) Deliberate omission, concealment,, or falsification of relevant facts from any personnel security form, personal history stamen or other form used to conduct investigations, determine employment qualifications, award benefits or status, determine security clearance eligibility or trustworthiness, or award fiduciary responsibilities, (b) Deliberately providing false or misleading information concerning relevant facts to an employer, investigator, security official, medical authority, or other official government representative, (c) Credible adverse information in several adjudicative issue areas that is not sufficient for an adverse determination under any other single guideline, but which, when considered as a whole, supports a whole-person assessment of questionable judgment, untrustworthiness, unreliability, lack of candor, unwillingness to comply with rules and regulations, or other characteristics indicating that the person may not properly safeguard protected information, (d) Credible adverse information that is not explicitly covered under any other guideline and may not be sufficient by itself for an adverse determination, but which, when combined with all available information supports a whole-person assessment of questionable judgment, untrustworthiness, unreliability, lack of candor, unwillingness to comply with rules and regulations, or other characteristics indicating that the person may not properly safeguard protected information. This includes but is not limited to consideration of: Untrustworthy/unreliable behavior (breach of client confidentiality, proprietary information, release of sensitive corporate or other government protected information) Disruptive, violent, or inappropriate workplace behavior, Pattern of dishonesty or rule violations, Evidence of significant misuse of government or other employer's time or resources, (e) Personal conduct or concealment of information about one's conduct, that creates a vulnerability to exploitation, manipulation, or duress, such as (1) engaging in activities which, if known, may affect the person's personal, professional, or community standing, or (2) while in another country, engaging in any activity that is illegal in that country or that is legal in that country but illegal in the United States and may serve as a basis for exploitation or pressure by the foreign security or intelligence service or other group, (f) Violation of a written or recorded commitment made by the individual to the employer as a condition of employment, (g) Association with persons involved in criminal activity.

Mitigating Conditions: (a) The individual made prompt, good-faith efforts to correct the omission, concealment, or falsification before being confronted with the facts, (b) Refusal or failure to cooperate, omission or concealment was caused or significantly contributed to by improper or inadequate advice of authorized personnel or legal counsel advising or instructing the individual specifically concerning the security clearance process. Upon being made aware of the requirement to cooperate or provide the information, the individual cooperated fully and truthfully, (c) Offense is so minor, or so much time has passed, or the behavior is so infrequent, or it happened under such unique circumstances that it is unlikely to recur and does not cast doubt on the individual's reliability, trustworthiness, or good judgment, occurred long ago, infrequently, or under unusual circumstances, (d) Individual has acknowledged the behavior and obtained counseling to change the behavior or taken other positive steps to alleviate the stressors, circumstances, or factors that caused untrustworthy, unreliable, or other inappropriate behavior, and such behavior is unlikely to recur, (e) Individual has taken positive steps to reduce or eliminate vulnerability to exploitation, manipulation, or duress, (f) Association with persons involved in criminal activities has ceased or occurs circumstances that do not cast doubt upon the individual's reliability, trustworthiness, judgment, or willingness to comply with rules and regulations

Guideline F – Financial Considerations

Concern: Failure or inability to live within one's means, satisfy debts, and meet financial obligations may indicate poor self-control, lack of judgment, or unwillingness to abide by rules and regulations, all of which can raise questions about an individual's reliability, trustworthiness and ability to protect classified information. An individual who is financially overextended is at risk of having to engage in illegal acts to generate funds. Compulsive gambling is a concern as it may lead to financial crimes including espionage. Affluence that cannot be explained by known sources of income is also a security concern. It may indicate proceeds from financially profitable criminal acts.

Disqualifying Conditions: (a) Inability or unwillingness to satisfy debts (b) Indebtedness caused by frivolous or irresponsible spending and the absence of any evidence of willingness or intent to pay the debt or establish a realistic plan to pay the debt. (c) A history of not meeting financial obligations, (d) Deceptive or illegal financial practices such as embezzlement, employee theft, check fraud, income tax evasion, expense account fraud, filing deceptive loan statements, and other intentional financial breaches of trust, (e) Consistent spending beyond one's means, which may be indicated by excessive indebtedness, significant negative cash flow, high debt-to-income ratio, and/or other financial analysis, (f) financial problems that are linked to drug abuse, alcoholism, gambling problems, or other issues of security concern, (g) failure to file annual Federal, state, or local income tax returns as required or the fraudulent filing of the same, (h) Unexplained affluence, as shown by a lifestyle or standard of living, increase in net worth, or money transfers that cannot be explained by subject's known legal sources of income, (i) Compulsive or addictive gambling as indicated by an unsuccessful attempt to stop gambling, "chasing losses", concealment of gambling losses, borrowing money to fund gambling or pay gambling debts, family conflict or other problems caused by gambling.

Mitigating Conditions: (a) Behavior happened so long ago, was so infrequent, or occurred under such circumstances that it is unlikely to recur and does not cast doubt on the individual's current reliability, trustworthiness, or good judgment occurred long ago, infrequently, or under unusual circumstances, (b) The conditions that resulted in the financial problem were largely beyond the person's control (e.g. loss of employment, a business downturn, unexpected medical emergency, or a death, divorce or separation), and the individual acted responsibly under the circumstances problem was beyond the individual's control, (c) Received or is receiving counseling for the problem and there are clear indications that the problem is being resolved or is under control, (d) Initiated a good-faith effort to repay overdue creditors or otherwise resolve debts, (e) Reasonable basis to dispute the legitimacy of the past-due debt which is the cause of the problem and provides documented proof to substantiate the basis of the dispute or provides evidence of actions to resolve the issue, (f) Affluence resulted from a legal source of income.

Guideline G – Alcohol Consumption

Concern: Excessive alcohol consumption often leads to the exercise of questionable judgment, unreliability, and failure to control impulses, and can raise questions about an individual's reliability and trustworthiness.

Disqualifying Conditions: (a) Alcohol-related incidents away from work, such as driving while under the influence, fighting, child or spouse abuse, disturbing the peace, or other incidents of concern, regardless of whether the individual is diagnosed as an alcohol abuser or alcohol dependent, (b) Alcohol-related incidents at work, such as reporting for work or duty in an intoxicated or impaired condition, or drinking on the job, regardless of whether the individual is diagnosed as an alcohol abuser or alcohol dependent, (c) Habitual or binge consumption of alcohol to the point of impaired judgment, regardless of whether the individual is diagnosed as an alcohol abuser or alcohol dependent, (d) Diagnosis by a duly qualified medical professional (e.g., physician, clinical psychologist, or psychiatrist) of alcohol abuse or alcohol dependence, (e) Evaluation of alcohol abuse or alcohol dependence by a licensed clinical social worker who is a staff member of a recognized alcohol treatment program, (f) Relapse after diagnosis of alcohol abuse or dependence and completion of an alcohol rehabilitation program, (g) Failure to follow court orders regarding alcohol education, evaluation, treatment, or abstinence

Mitigating Conditions: (a) So much time has passed, or the behavior was so infrequent, or it happened under such unusual circumstances that it is unlikely to recur or does not cast doubt on current reliability, trustworthiness, or good judgment, (b) Acknowledges his or her alcoholism or issues of alcohol abuse, provides evidence of actions taken to overcome this problem, and has established a pattern of abstinence (if alcohol dependent) or responsible use (if an alcohol abuser);Individual has acknowledged and overcome problem, (c) Individual is a current employee who is participating in a counseling or treatment program, has no history of previous treatment and relapse, and is making satisfactory progress, (d) individual has successfully completed inpatient or outpatient counseling or rehabilitation along with any required aftercare, has demonstrated a clear and established pattern of modified consumption or abstinence in accordance with treatment recommendations, such as participation in meetings of Alcoholics Anonymous or a similar organization and has received a favorable prognosis by a duly qualified medical professional or a licensed clinical social worker who is a staff member of a recognized alcohol treatment program.

Guideline H – Drug Involvement

Concern: The use of illegal drugs or misuse of prescription drugs can raise questions about an individual's reliability and trustworthiness, both because drug use may impair judgment and because it raises questions about an individual's willingness to comply with laws, rules, and regulations.

Disqualifying Conditions (a) Any drug abuse, (b) Testing positive for an illegal drug, (c) Illegal drug possession, including cultivation, processing, manufacture, purchase, sale, or distribution; or possession of drug paraphernalia, (d) Diagnosis of drug abuse or dependence by a duly qualified medical professional (e.g., physician, clinical psychologist, or psychiatrist) (e) Evaluation of drug abuse or drug dependence by a licensed clinical social worker who is a staff member of a recognized drug treatment program, (f) Failure to successfully complete a drug treatment program prescribed by a duly qualified medical professional, (g) Any illegal drug use after being granted a security clearance, (h) Expressed intent to continue illegal drug use, failure to clearly and convincingly commit to discontinue, illegal drug use.

Mitigating Conditions: (a) Behavior happened so long ago, was so infrequent, or happened under such circumstances that it is unlikely to recur or does not cast doubt on the individual's current reliability, trustworthiness, or good judgment, (b) A demonstrated intent not to abuse any drugs in the future, such as: Dissociation from drug-using associates and contacts, changing or avoiding the environment where drugs were used, an appropriate period of abstinence, signed statement of intent with automatic revocation of clearance for any violation, (c) abuse of prescription drugs was after a severe or prolonged illness during which these drugs were prescribed, and abuse has since ended, (d) satisfactory completion of drug treatment program including but not limited to rehabilitation and aftercare requirements, without recurrence of abuse, and a favorable prognosis by a duly qualified medical professional.

Guideline I – Psychological Conditions

Concern: Certain emotional, mental, and personality conditions can impair judgment, reliability, or trustworthiness. A formal diagnosis of a disorder is not required for there to be a concern under this guideline. A duly qualified mental health professional (e.g., clinical psychologist or psychiatrist) employed by, or acceptable to and approved by the U.S. Government, should be consulted when evaluating potentially disqualifying and mitigating information under this guideline. No negative inference concerning the standards in this Guideline may be raised solely on the basis of seeking mental health counseling.

Disqualifying Conditions: (a) Behavior that casts doubt on judgment, reliability, or trustworthiness that is not covered under any other guideline but not limited to emotionally unstable, irresponsible, dysfunctional, violent, paranoid, or bizarre behavior, (b) An opinion by a duly qualified mental health professional that the individual has a condition not covered under any other guideline that may impair judgment, reliability, or trustworthiness, (c) Failure to follow treatment advice related to a diagnosed emotional, mental, or personality condition, e.g. failure to take prescribed medication.

Mitigating Conditions: (a) The identified condition is readily controllable with treatment, and the individual has demonstrated ongoing and consistent compliance with the treatment plan, (b) Individual has voluntarily entered a counseling or treatment program for a condition that is amenable to treatment, and the individual is currently receiving counseling or treatment with a favorable prognosis by a duly qualified mental health professional, (c) Recent opinion by a duly qualified mental health professional employed by, or acceptable to and approved by the U.S. Government that an individual's previous condition is under control or in remission, and has a low probability of recurrence or exacerbation, (d) The past emotional instability was a temporary condition (e.g., one caused by a death, illness, or marital breakup), the situation has been resolved, and the individual no longer shows indications of emotional instability, (e) There is no indication of a current problem.

Guideline J – Criminal Conduct

Concern: Criminal activity creates doubt about a person's judgment, reliability, and trustworthiness and calls into question a person's ability or willingness to comply with laws, rules, and regulations.

Disqualifying Conditions: (a) Single serious crime or multiple lesser offenses, (b) Dishonorable discharge or dismissal from Armed Forces under less than honorable conditions, (c) Allegation or admission of criminal conduct, regardless of whether the person was formally charged, formally prosecuted or convicted Ü (d) Individual currently on parole or probation, (e) Violation of parole or probation, or failure to complete a court-mandated rehabilitation program.

Mitigating Conditions: (a) So much time has elapsed since the criminal behavior happened, or it happened under such unusual circumstances that it is unlikely to recur or does not cast doubt on the individual's reliability, trustworthiness, or good judgment, (b) The person was pressured or coerced into committing the act and those pressures are no longer present in the person's life, (c) Evidence that the person did not commit the offense, (d) There is evidence of successful rehabilitation; including but not limited to the passage of time without recurrence of criminal activity, remorse or restitution, job training or higher education, good employment record, or constructive community involvement

Guideline K – Handling Protected Information

Concern: Deliberate or negligent failure to comply with rules and regulations for protecting classified or other sensitive information raises doubt about an individual's trustworthiness, judgment, reliability, or willingness and ability to safeguard such information and is a serious security concern.

Disqualifying Conditions: (a) Deliberate or negligent disclosure of classified or other protected information to unauthorized persons, including but not limited to personal or business contacts, to the media, or to persons present at seminars, meetings, or conferences, (b) Collecting or storing classified or other protected information in any unauthorized location, (c) Loading, drafting, editing, modifying, storing, transmitting, or otherwise handling classified reports, data, or other information on any unapproved equipment including but not limited to any typewriter, word processor, or computer hardware, software, drive, system, game board, handheld, "palm" or pocket device or other adjunct equipment, (d) Inappropriate efforts to obtain or view classified or other protected information outside one's need to know, (e) Copying classified or other protected information in a manner designed to conceal or remove classification or other document control markings, (f) Viewing or downloading information from a secure system when the information is beyond the individual's need to know, (g) Any failure to comply with rules for the protection of classified or other sensitive information, (h) Negligence or lax security habits that persist despite counseling by management, (i) Failure to comply with rules or regulations that results in damage to the National Security, regardless of whether it was deliberate or negligent.

Mitigating Conditions: (a) So much time has elapsed since the behavior, or it happened so infrequently or under such unusual circumstances that it is unlikely to recur or does not cast doubt on the individual's current reliability, trustworthiness, or good judgment, (b) Individual responded favorably to counseling or remedial security training and now demonstrates a positive attitude toward the discharge of security responsibilities, (c) Security violations were due to improper or inadequate training.

Guideline L – Outside Activities

Concern: Involvement in certain types of outside employment or activities is of security concern if it poses a conflict of interest with an individual's security responsibilities and could create an increased risk of unauthorized disclosure of classified.

Disqualifying Conditions: (a) Any employment or service, whether compensated or volunteer, with the government of: a foreign country or any foreign national, organization, or other entity, a representative of any foreign interest, any foreign, domestic, or international organization or person engaged in analysis, discussion, or publication of material on intelligence, defense, foreign affairs, or protected technology organization that analyzes, discusses, or publishes material on intelligence, defense, foreign affairs, or protected technology organization that analyzes, discusses, or publishes material (b) Failure to report or fully disclose an outside activity when this is required.

Mitigating Conditions: (a) Evaluation of the outside employment or activity by the appropriate security or counterintelligence office indicates that it does not pose a conflict with an individual's security responsibilities or with the national security interests of the United States, (b) The individual terminates the employment or discontinued the activity upon being notified that it was in conflict with his or her security responsibilities.

Guideline M – Misuse of Information Technology

Concern: Noncompliance with rules, procedures, guidelines or regulations pertaining to information technology systems may raise security concerns about an individual's reliability and trustworthiness, calling into question the willingness or ability to properly protect sensitive systems, networks, and information. Information Technology Systems include all related computer hardware, software, firmware, and data used for the communication, transmission, processing, manipulation, storage, or protection of information.

Disqualifying Conditions: (a) Illegal or unauthorized entry into any information technology system or component, (b) illegal or unauthorized modification, destruction, manipulation or denial of access to information, software, firmware, or hardware in an information technology system, (c) use of any information technology system to gain unauthorized access to another system or to a compartmented area within the same system, (d) downloading, storing, or transmitting classified information on or to any unauthorized software, hardware, or information technology system, (e) unauthorized use of a government or other information technology system, (f) introduction, removal, or duplication of hardware, firmware, software, or media to or from any information technology system without authorization, when prohibited by rules, procedures, guidelines or regulations, (g) Negligence or lax security habits in handling information technology that persist despite counseling by management, (h) Any misuse of information technology, whether deliberate or negligent, that results in damage to the national security. [114]

---

[114] *The 13 Adjudicative Guidelines*, Center for Development of Security Excellence, April 2015. Retrieved 26 Nov, 2019, https://www.cdse.edu/documents/cdse/job-aid-13-adjudicative-guidelines-v2.pdf

SOURCES

CHAPTER ONE OVERVIEW

Greg Botelho and Joe Sterling.. FBI: Navy Yard shooter 'delusional,' said 'low frequency attacks' drove him to kill. *CNN* September 26, 2013.

Internal review of the Washington Navy Yard Shooting, A Report to the Secretary of Defense, 20 Nov, 2013, P 3. https://apps.dtic.mil/dtic/tr/fulltext/u2/a602573.pdf https://edition.cnn.com/2013/09/25/us/washington-navy-yard-investigation/

Earley, P (1997) *Confessions of a Spy*, Putnam & Sons, NY.

https://www.bing.com/images/search?q=teddy+roosevelt+quotes+arena&qs=CustomSearch&pq=teddy+roosevelt+quotes&sc=3-22&cvid=ADB8674BD43245A499CBA820BA0C48BA&sp=3&form=QBIR

Weiner, Tim; Johnston, David; Lewis, Neil A. (1995). *Betrayal: The Story of Aldrich Ames, an American Spy*. New York: Random House.

Wohlstetter, R, (1962) *Pearl Harbor: Warning and Decision*, Stanford University Press, CA.

Fitzgerald, J, (2014) *Journey to the Center of the Mind*, West Conshohocken, PA.

Thompson, T. (2006) *Why Espionage Happens*, Seaboard Press, Florence SC, First edition.

CHAPTER TWO THE BACKGROUND INVESTIGATION

Henderson, W, *Security Clearance Investigations Process Updated*, 9 Oct 2011, Clearance Jobs, https://news.clearancejobs.com/2011/10/09/security-clearance- investigations-process-updated/

Homicide Watch, DOD Report 18 March 2014, *Navy Yard Shooting: DOD Missed Warning Signs, Report Says*, http://homicidewatch.org/2014/03/18/navy-yard-shooting-dod- missed-warning-signs-report-says/

Wise, D. (1988) *The Spy Who Got Away*, Random House, NY.

Enhanced the Productivity and Scope of Background Investigations (1996, 1991) PERSEREC, Monterey CA. https://www.dhra.mil/PERSEREC/Past-Achievements/#BIs

U.S. Department of Labor Web Page, Wage and Hour Division, *Employee Polygraph Protection Act (EPPA) Overview*, https://www.dol.gov/whd/polygraph/

Earley, P, (1988) *Family of Spies*, Bantam Books, NY.

Security Executive Agent Directive 5, Clapper, J, 12 May 2016.

Wells G. & Needleham, S, *Florida Shooter: When Social Media Foretells a Mass Shooting*, Wall Street Journal, 16 Feb 2018, https://www.wsj.com/articles/when-social-media-foretells-a-mass- shooting-1518802803

Abrams, S, (1989) *The Complete Polygraph Handbook*, Lexington Books, Lexington Mass.

Krogsbøll, L, physician, Jørgensen, KJ, physician, Larsen, CJ, physician, Gøtzsche, P. *General health checks in adults for reducing morbidity and mortality from disease*: Cochrane systematic review and meta-analysis, Nov, 2012, BMJ 2012; 345:e7191.

Haidt, J & Lukianoff, G, (2018) *The Coddling of the American Mind*, Penguin Books, NY.

Ropeik, D, (2010) *How Risky is it, Really?* McGraw Hill, NY.

Finucane, M.L.; Alhakami, A.; Slovic, P.; Johnson, S.M. (January 2000). *The Affect Heuristic in Judgment of Risks and Benefits*. Journal of Behavioral Decision Making. 13 (1): 1–17

CHAPTER FOUR ADJUDICATIONS

Center for the Development of Security Excellence, *DoD Security Specialist Course: Personnel Security*.

911 Commission Report, Norton & Co, NYC.

Associated Press, Washington Times, P A-8, 30 August 20

FBI Uniform Crime Reporting Statistics, 2015, *Crime in the United States, 2015*, https://ucr.fbi.gov/crime-in-the-u.s/2015/crime-in-the- u.s.-2015/tables/table-42

Loesche, D, *The Prison Gender Gap*, Statista, 23 Oct 2017, https://www.statista.com/chart/11573/gender-of-inmates-in-us- federal-prisons-and-general-population/

CHAPTER FIVE PSYCHOLOGY AND PERSONNEL SECURITY

Festinger, L. (1957) *A Theory of Cognitive Dissonance*, Stanford University Press, Ca.

Esgate, A. Groome, D. (2005). *An Introduction to Applied Cognitive Psychology*. Psychology Press. p. 201.

Cherry, K, *The Affect Heuristic and Decision Making*, Verywell mind, 13 Aug 2019, https://www.verywellmind.com/what-is-the-affect- heuristic-2795028

Cherry, *Understanding the Optimism Bias AKA the Illusion of Invulnerability* 12 Aug, 2019 https://www.verywellmind.com/what-is-the-optimism-bias-2795031

Nofsinger, J. Ph.D. *Familiarity Bias PART I: What is it?* Psychology Today, 25 July 2008, https://www.psychologytoday.com/intl/blog/mind-my- money/200807/familiarity-bias-part-i-what-is-it

Urbina, S & Anastasi, A. (1997). *Psychological testing (7th ed.)* Upper Saddle River, NJ: Prentice Hall

Trzepacz, PT & Baker RW (1993). *The Psychiatric Mental Status Examination.* Oxford, U.K.: Oxford University Press.

Framingham, J, Ph.D. *The Minnesota Multiphasic Personality Inventory (MMPI)* Psych Central, https://psychcentral.com/lib/minnesota-multiphasic-personality- inventory-mmpi/

Thiessen, M, (2010) *Courting Disaster*, Regnery Publishing, NY, NY

Chow, S, Ph.D. *Peptic Ulcer History*, News, Medical Life Sciences, 23 Aug 2018, Retrieved, 18 Sept 2019, https://www.news- medical.net/health/Peptic-Ulcer-History.aspx

Huston, M, *Notes from a Revolution*, Psychology Today, May/June 2019

CHAPTER SIX PERSONNEL SECURITY AND CATASTROPHIC EVENTS

Spitzer, R, Interview on All Things Considered, Michel Martin, *The Relationship Between Domestic Violence And Mass Shootings*, 7 Oct 2017.

Levinson, E, Pagliery, J & De Puy Camp, M, *Thousand Oaks shooter was a Marine veteran who often visited the site of the shooting*, CNN Online, 8 Nov 2018.

Loanes, E, *Police call Florida shooter's social media presence 'disturbing'* The Daily Dot, 16 Feb, 2018. https://www.dailydot.com/layer8/florida-shooters-disturbing-social- media-presence/

Reed, T, 19 Sept 2007, AP, *Ex-Astronaut Wants Evidence Tossed Out*, https://web.archive.org/web/20071026011659/http://apnews.mywa y.com/article/20070919/D8ROJMJ00.html

Clearance Jobs.com. *Psychological Health Question Has Changed in SF-86 Questionnaire*, https://www.keepyourclearance.com/news/sf- 86-psychological-health-question-has-changed/

Veterans Law Group, https://search.yahoo.com/search?p=veteranslaw.com&fr=uh-mail- web&fr2=p%3AmI%2Cm%3Asb.

CHAPTER SEVEN RISKS, PERCENTAGES, PROBABILITIES AND PROPORTIONALITY

Ropeik, D. (2010) *How Risky is it, Really?* McGraw Hill, NY.

Kahneman, D. (2011) *Thinking Fast and Slow*, Farrar, Straus & Giroux, NY.

Internal Review of the Washington Navy Yard Shooting, *A Report to the Secretary of Defense*, 20 Nov, 2013. https://archive.defense.gov/pubs/Navy-Investigation-into-the-WNY- Shooting_final-report.pdf

CHAPTER EIGHT SUBSTANCE USE AND ABUSE

DSM IV TR, American Psychiatric Association, Arlington VA, 2005.

NY Dailey News Headline *I am a Rat*, page 1, 6 March, 1992, https://www.gettyimages.com/detail/news-photo/daily-news-front- page-march-6-sammy-bull-im-a-rat-gravano-news-photo/97298862

Raddan-Keith, P, *Assets and Liabilities*, The New Yorker, 21 Sept 2005 https://www.newyorker.com/magazine/2015/09/21/assets- and- liabilities

Clapper, J, *Adherence to Federal Laws Prohibiting Marijuana Use*, 25 Oct 2014. https://www.employmentlawobserver.com/assets/htmldocuments/ Blogs/EmploymentLawObserver/dni-memo-20fed-laws-prohibiting- marijuana-use.pdf

Veterans Cannabis Use for Safe Healing Act Cosponsor: 10/15/2019: Rep. Neguse, Joe [D-CO-2]

Web MD, *Is medical marijuana FDA approved?* 15 Dec 2018, https://www.webmd.com/a-to-z- guides/qa/is-medical- marijuana- fda-approved

Center for Disease Control and Prevention (CDC) National Center for Health Statistics, 1999-2017, Retrieved 24 Oct 2019, https://en.wikipedia.org/wiki/Opioid_epidemic_in_the_United_State

Food and Drug Administration home page, *Timeline of Selected FDA Activities and Significant Events Addressing Opioid Misuse and Abuse*, 25 Sept 2019 https://www.fda.gov/drugs/information-drug- class/timeline-selected-fda-activities-and-significant-events- addressing-opioid-misuse-and-abuse

Noble, M, Treadwell, J. R, Tregear, S. J, Coates, V. H, Wiffen, P. J., Akafomo, C, Schoelles, K. M. (2010). Noble, Meredith (ed.). *Long- term opioid management for chronic noncancer pain.* Cochrane Database of Systematic Reviews (1): CD006605.

T, Buddy, *The Combination of Domestic Abuse and Alcohol*, 18 Sept 2019, The Very Well Mind, https://www.verywellmind.com/domestic-abuse-and-alcohol-62643

National Institute on Drug Abuse, No author, *Substance Abuse in the Military*, Oct 2019, https://www.drugabuse.gov/publications/drugfacts/substance- abuse-in-military

Bing Images, *Age and Drug Use*, Oct, 2019 https://www.bing.com/images/search?q=age+and+drug+use&qpvt= age+and+drug+use&form=IGRE&first=1&cw=1129&ch=473

Carne, T, (2019) *Alienated America*, Harper Collins, NY

CHAPTER NINE FINANCES

Wikipedia, https://en.wikipedia.org/wiki/Household_debt

Boundy, D. (1993). *When money is the drug, The compulsion for credit cash and chronic debt.* Harper Collins, NY.

Thompson, T (2009) *Why Espionage Happens*, Seaboard Press, South Carolina.

Lindgren, H, (1991) *The Psychology of Money*, Kreiger & Co, NY.

Henriques, Diana (2011) *The Wizard of Lies*, Holt, NY.

Thompson, T, (2015) *Common Sense Psychology*, America Star Books, Baltimore.

Shaffer, H, Hall, M, Vander Bilt, J, (September 1999). *Estimating the Prevalence of Disordered Gambling Behavior in the United States and Canada: A Research Synthesis.* American Journal of Public Health. 89 (9)

Affidavit, U.S. District Court, U.S. versus Brian Regan, Alexandria VA, Feb, 2002

CHAPTER TEN OTHER ADJUDICATIVE ISSUES

Lopez, G, *Why you can't blame mass incarceration on the war on drugs,* Vox, 30 May 2017, https://www.vox.com/policy-and- politics/2017/5/30/15591700/mass-incarceration-john-pfaff-locked- in

Adjudicator Desk Reference, 2007 statistics, PERSEREC, https://www.dhra.mil/portals/52/documents/perserec/adr_version_4.pdf

Bureau of Justice Statistics. (2001). *Nature and distribution of known offenses.* In Sourcebook of Criminal Justice Statistics, 2001. Washington, DC: U.S. Department of Justice.

Pew Research, *Social & Demographic Trends, Millennials in Adulthood,* 7 March 2014, https://www.pewsocialtrends.org/2014/03/07/millennials-in- adulthood/

Center for the Development of Security Excellence, *Job Aid 13: Adjudicative Guidelines,* April 2015. https://www.cdse.edu/documents/cdse/job-aid-13-adjudicative- guidelines-v2.pdf

Chelsea Manning, WIKIPEDIA, 14 Nov 2019

CIA Inspector *General Report,* Snider, L.B. 18 Feb, 2000, https://fas.org/irp/cia/product/ig_deutch.html

Sniffen, MJ, *Ex-CIA Head Planned Guilty Plea,* Washington Post, 24 Jan 2001. http://www.washingtonpost.com/wp- srv/aponline/20010124/aponline163741_000.htm

Duncan, I, Baltimore Sun, Baltimore estimates cost of ransomware attack at $18.2 million as government begins to restore email accounts, 29 May 2019, https://www.baltimoresun.com/maryland/baltimore-city/bs-md-ci- ransomware-email-20190529-story.html

Winch, G, (2018) *How to Fix Broken Heart*, Simon & Schuster, NY.

Kalugin, O, Former Soviet KGB Officer, Texas A & M conference, 1999.

Herbig, K, PERSEREC, *Changes in Espionage by Americans: 1947-2007*, March 2008. https://www.dhra.mil/Portals/52/Documents/perserec/tr08-05.pdf

Charney, D & Ervin, J, *The Psychology of Espionage*, The Intelligencer, Vol 22 No. 1, Spring 2016.

Leipholtz, B, The Fix, *World Health Organization Adds Sex Addiction to Disease List*, 17 July, 2018, https://www.thefix.com/world-health- organization-adds-sex-addiction-disease-list

www.ingramcontent.com/pod-product-compliance
Lightning Source LLC
Chambersburg PA
CBHW050217230526
45470CB00001B/425